Guide to the

Borghese Gallery

edited by

Kristina Herrmann Fiore

A VISIT TO THE BORGHESE GALLERY

The Villa Pinciana within the context of Pope Paul V's town-planning policy

"Outside Porta Pinciana he had a beautiful palace built in one of his Vineyards, or Gardens or Villas, however we wish to call it, in which every delight we might desire or have in this life was to be found. It was entirely adorned with beautiful antique and modern statues, fine paintings, and other precious things, including fountains, fishponds and embellishments ..." This is how G. Baglione, a painter and art critic of the period, described Pope Paul V's (1605-1621) urban innovations, but he also added that this Borghese Pope "aimed at beautifying the City of Rome and in doing so glorified his name." In fact Paul V's urban improvements in Rome can be compared to those of the better-known Sixtus V. During his pontificate, many old façades of pre-existing buildings were restored, as

M. Provenzale, *Portrait of Paul V*, 1621

in the case of St. Peter's, and squares and fountains were created in front of them. The Cappella Paulina, the great construction of the sacristy and the column of the Madonna in the square before it were added to the basilica of S. Maria Maggiore. The Quirinal and Vatican palaces were also enlarged. Flaminio Ponzio designed the Palazzo Borghese at Ripetta, the so-called Cembalo Borghese, and added considerable extensions. This communicated with a square decorated with a central fountain and surrounded by balustrades surmounted by antique statues, similar to the one he was to design a few years later for the Villa Borghese. Because of his interest in water systems and fountains, Paul V was nicknamed *Fontefice Massimo*; he restored the aqueduct built by the Emperor Augustus on the Via Aurelia and commissioned an imposing theatrical fountain on the Janiculum, known as the Acqua Paola and designed

P. Brill, *View of a Port* c.1607

by Flaminio Ponzio. The most innovative aspect of the Borghese town-planning policy was the orientation of the architecture and façades towards the exterior and hence their greater involvement in the urban surroundings and squares by means of porticoes, staircases and fountains.

Pope Paul V's pontificate was marked by the consolidation and rigorous reform of ecclesiastical power, which aimed at worldwide evangelization. Diplomatic relations between the Holy See and all the continents, even as far away as Japan, are still reflected in the wall paintings (executed by A. Tassi, G. Lanfranco and C. Saraceni in 1616-1617) in the Sala Regia in the Quirinal Palace, which depict the ambassadors of those distant lands paying homage to Paul V. The Pope's position in Europe was distinguished by an impartial commitment to keep the peace between the reigning powers, particularly between the Hapsburgs and the Bourbons. In the fifteenth year of his pontificate, Paul V, a jurist by education and family tradition, made rigorous use of his training to underline the absolute sovereignty of the temporal power of the Catholic Church, by defending ecclesiastical immunity and Doctrine, thus stimulating the opposition of the Republic of Venice, home of Fra Paolo Sarpi, and conflicting with the research methods Galileo Galilei was advocating. As regards the Church's internal controversies, particularly between

Dominicans and Jesuits, concerning the nature of 'divine Grace', Paul V managed to re-establish a certain balance by refusing to allow either of the theories to prevail. The compulsory requirement that bishops reside in their dioceses and the drafting of the *Rituale Romanum*, regulated procedures. Paul V confirmed the *Officium* for the cult of Guardian Angels (1612), beatified Philip Neri, Theresa of Ávila, Ignatius Loyola, Francis Xavier and canonized Carlo Borromeo, Francesca Romana and Thomas of Villanova.

Cardinal Scipione Borghese, nephew of the Pope

What we would call today cultural policy at the papal court or diplomatic and ceremonial relations were entrusted to the Pope's favourite nephew, Cardinal Scipione Caffarelli Borghese. Two months after his uncle had been elected, twenty-six-year-old Scipione, son of the Pope's sister Ortensia Borghese and Francesco Caffarelli, was made a cardinal and generously rewarded. During his ecclesiastical career he was appointed Papal Legate in Avignon, Archpriest of the Lateran, Prefect of the Congregation of the Council, Abbot of S. Gregorio al Celio, Librarian of the Holy Roman Church, Grand Penitentiary, Camerlengo (or Papal Chamberlain) and Prefect of the Apostolic Briefs, Prefect of the Segnatura of Grace, Archbishop of Bologna, Archpriest of St. Peter's, Protector of the Holy House of Loreto, Protector of Flanders and Germany as well as of the Dominican and Camaldolese orders. Cardinal Scipione possessed an infallible instinct for rec-

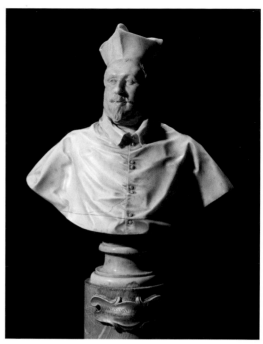

G. L. Bernini, *Cardinal Scipione Borghese*, c.1632

ognizing artistic quality and driven by a ruthless passion he used fair means or foul to acquire the most prized works of art. He drew public attention to himself by his unscrupulous actions both as collector and client, by his shrewd patronage of outstanding talents (we need only mention Gian Lorenzo Bernini, Nicolas Cordier, Caravaggio, Domenichino, Guido Reni and Rubens) and by building the extraordinary Villa Borghese, in which the three arts, sculpture, painting and architecture, vie with nature.

The Villa Pinciana was considerably smaller than the imposing Villa Aldobrandini at Frascati, as the biographer Bzovius pointed out in his life of Pope Paul V, in 1624, "*non ad pompam exteriorem, neque ad ostentationem puerilem*". But the influence of Scipione Borghese and of his villa extended far beyond the

Marcantonio I Borghese (1504-1574), m. Flaminia Astalli

Camillo
1552-1621
Cardinal 1596
Pope Paul V, 1605

Francesco
1557-1620
General of Holy
Roman Church
m. Ortensia Santacroce

Giambattista
1558-1609
Commander of
Castel S. Angelo
m. Virginia Lante

Ortensia
1561-1598
m. Francesco Caffarelli

Marcantonio II
1601-1658
Prince
m. Camilla Orsini (1619)

Scipione
Borghese Caffarelli
1579-1633
Cardinal
1605

Paolo
1624-1646
m. Olimpia Aldobrandini, 1638

Giovanni Battista
1639-1717
m. Eleonora Boncompagni

Marcantonio III
1660-1729
Viceroy of Naples
m. Flaminia Spinola

Camillo
1693-1763
m. Agnese Colonna

Marcantonio IV
1730-1800
m. Anna Maria Salviati, 1768

Camillo
1775-1832
m. Pauline Bonaparte, 1803

Francesco Aldobrandini
1776-1839
Borghese from 1832
m. Adélaïde de la Rochefoucauld

Marcantonio V
1814-1886
m. Guendalina Talbot
and m. Thérèse de la Rochefoucauld

Paolo
1845-1920
m. Elena Appony

very high quality of his collection of ancient and modern works of art. He promoted a style that was new yet antique, serene, harmonious and tangibly close to the spectator. 'His' sculptors, painters and architects were to launch Roman Baroque, which would be imitated throughout Europe.

The Borghese family and the villa until 1901

By the beginning of the 17th century, the Borghese family had become famous in Rome for their architectural projects, their monumental inscriptions, their heraldic symbols of the eagle and the dragon on façades, fountains and portals, and in particular for the Villa Pinciana. The family, however, had played a dominant role in Tuscany, and especially in Siena, for at least three centuries. The Emperor Sigismund conferred a knighthood on Agostino Borghese and granted him the privilege of including the eagle in his coat of arms, for having defended the Imperial Party in 1433. Marcantonio Borghese moved to Rome in 1547, after being appointed Consistorial Lawyer. He was followed by his relatives in 1554, after Siena came under Medici domination. His daughter Ortensia married Duke Francesco Caffarelli. Evidence that the family had settled in Rome can be seen from the fact that in 1578 they possessed a private chapel in the church of Trinità dei Monti. Ortensia's brother, Camillo Borghese, later Pope Paul V (1605-1621), cardinal since 1596, Apostolic Delegate in Spain and Vicar-General of the Church, who owned a dignified house in Via dell'Orso,

bought a large palazzo (begun by the architect Martino Longhi il Vecchio and extended by Ponzio) at Ripetta in 1605. But he soon gave it to his brothers, Giovanni Battista, Gonfalonier of the Holy Roman Church, and Francesco, Commander of the Papal Galleys. In 1609, Cardinal Scipione bought a palace near St. Peter's (now the Palazzo Giraud Torlonia in Via della Conciliazione). This became the first home of his already considerable art collection that was to be transferred to the new villa outside Porta Pinciana in the 1620s. A villa which would be linked to the Borghese family for the following three centuries. In 1633, Cardinal Scipione instituted a *fideicommissum* or deed of trust in order to preserve his collection intact.

Between 1770 and 1800, Marcantonio IV Borghese was responsible for the second stage of alterations to the villa. He modernized not only the extensive

A. Canova, *Pauline Bonaparte*, 1805-1808

gardens but also the villa's interior by introducing architectural designs of rare Neoclassical beauty, which harmonized with the measured late Baroque style, the work of the brilliant architect Antonio Asprucci. The ceilings and walls were decorated with paintings and stuccoes by outstanding Italian and foreign artists (painters Mariano Rossi, Domenico de Angelis, Tommaso Conca, Cristoforo Unterberger, Anton von Maron, Gavin Hamilton, Pietro Antonio Novelli, Domenico Corvi, Giuseppe Cades, Felice Giani, Giovanni Battista Marchetti, Wenzel Peters and sculptors Luigi Valadier, Vincenzo Pacetti, Agostino Penna, Maximilien Laboureur, Francesco Carradori and others). In 1798, as a result of the Treaty of Tolentino, Marcantonio IV Borghese was forced to send his best paintings to France. The works by Raphael and Domenichino were the most esteemed by French revolutionary taste and the packing cases containing *The Deposition* and the *Diana* were marked with high-sounding inscriptions praising these two illustrious representatives of Roman painting as they made their triumphal entry into Paris. Marcantonio IV's son, Camillo Borghese, had been a Jacobin and was to play a role in Napoleon's political chess game by marrying the emperor's sister, Pauline Bonaparte. He was later forced to 'sell' 344 pieces from his archaeological collection, which still constitute the 'Borghese Collection' in the Louvre. But it was in Paris, in 1827, that Camillo Borghese purchased Correggio's *Danäe*.

In the 1830s, the architect Luigi Canino designed a project for the extension of the park for Prince Camillo (including the purchase of land up to Piazza del Popolo) and he renovated the Palazzina, which had been sadly despoiled of the statues and reliefs that had decorated its exterior. The *fideicommissum* had been annulled because of the revolution, but was later re-established in 1816 with a *motu proprio* by Pius VII, for whom Prince Francesco Borghese made an inventory, in 1833, of the paintings and sculptures unquestionably housed in the Palazzo and the Villa Borghese, to prevent any further dispersal of his legacy. At the end of the 19th century, when building speculation in the Ludovisi area of the city had disastrous consequences for the family finances, Prince Paolo was forced to sell the Villa Borghese to the Italian state. After lengthy negotiations parliament authorized the purchase in December 1901; in July 1902, the park, the buildings and all the works of art were bought for the sum of a mere 3,600,000 Lire. In 1903, the park was handed over to the Rome City Council, while the Palazzina and art collection remained state property. The immediate consequence of this division of the estate was the demolition, in 1906, of the walls surrounding the secret gardens, formerly used for the cultivation of rare plants, which, since the time of Cardinal Scipione, had formed an integral part of the architecture and vistas of the villa. The Borghese family tree shows the various figures who have played a major role in the history of the Villa Borghese.

The architecture of the villa

The Villa Pinciana was built as a museum to house fine examples of ancient

Interior of Room IV

and modern art, as a music and centre, but also as a place for the contemplation of nature (in the form of rare plants and animals), of fossil specimens and of the modern technology of the time, i.e. automata, mirrors, bizarre lenses and special clocks. Like a 'Theatre of the Universe' the purpose of the works of art in this museum was to influence taste and recreation - a concept far-removed from that of the encyclopaedic museums in the following century. All this is reflected in the rational design of the villa which radiates light.

The architecture, inspired by ancient Roman villas, also had to be in keeping with its function as the diplomatic seat of the papal court, by giving the impression of a revival of Roman magnificence. In 1616, the Japanese ambassador was given a sumptuous banquet there "after which he departed most satisfied", though he did not succeed in obtaining any political support. The villa administered a large farm with vineyards, vegetable gardens, hunting grounds, stables, barns, dovecotes in the towers (whose entrances are still visible), a large aviary, an ice store, a wine cellar and even silkworms. Extremely rare plants imported from Holland and the Indies and a zoological garden completed Cardinal Scipione's 'Theatre of the Universe' The 'public' nature of this park with its statues and fountains and its permanent open-air exhibition of ancient sculptures was underlined by a Latin inscription which Cardinal Scipione set on the front of the small theatre in the park, near the zoological garden. [1] However, as early as 1621, the year of the Pope's death, Cardinal Scipione

C. Deruet, *The Assumption*, 1617-1618

L. and G. Valadier, *Fireplace*, 1786

was obliged to record the high cost of the "soldiers employed to guard the Villa Pinciana".

The architecture of the villa, with its two towers, portico and large entrance hall, resembles that of 16th-century suburban villas and particularly the Villa Farnesina and the Villa Medici, Villas Ruffina and Mondragone at Frascati, and last but not least, the Villa Montalto Peretti (1588), designed to house an art collection and set in a garden in the area of the present-day Piazza dei Cinquecento.

The addition of ancient sculptures to the façade stems from a tradition developed by Roman collectors, who used them first to decorate the courtyards and later the façades of their palazzi (for instance, Palazzo della Valle 1517, Palazzo Gaddi 1538, Palazzo Spada 1555, Pope Pius IV's casino 1558-1561 in the Vatican gardens, Villa Medici c.1580 and Palazzo Matteo di

Berrettini, *Ceiling of Room XI with the Myth of Ganymede*

Giove 1598-1611). Already in Raphael's day, the public nature of the 'exhibition of ancient sculpture and Roman history' was common on numerous façades painted by Polidoro and Maturino that displayed antique reliefs and statues. In the case of the more severe Villa Medici (Annibale Lippi 1564 and Alberto Alberti c.1580) the façade, rich in antique statues and reliefs faced the garden, whereas Cardinal Scipione's villa welcomed the visitor with its spacious forecourt.

The typical 'antique-style suburban villa' was not only richly decorated with statues and Doric orders, but also pale in colour, thus evoking the white marble façades of the Rome which the Emperor Augustus transformed from a city of brick into one of marble. Particular attention was paid to the perspectival relationships between the exterior and interior of the villa, to the axial layout of the sequence of rooms and the avenues in the garden, as well as to the interplay between the statues and balustrades in the forecourt and those on the façade. The arrangement of the large windows (four of which have been recently restored) and the original architecture of light still enhances the viewing of the works of art today.

Formerly access to the portico was by a double staircase, which was a deliberate imitation of Michelangelo's staircase leading to the Palazzo del Senatore on the Capitol. In the late 18th century the staircase was demolished because its foundations were giving way and was replaced by an inappropriate pyramidal staircase. On the basis of the detailed measurements in the accounts of the stonemasons who built the 17th-century staircase, which are to be found in a large volume in the Vatican Secret Archives (casa Borghese vol. 4174), in

1994, Prof. G. Ioppolo designed a project for the reconstruction of the original staircase by Flaminio Ponzio. [2]

After the purchase of land and vineyards and the concession of water from the Acqua Felice aqueduct in the first decade of the 17th century, work on the construction of the palace began in 1612 and was virtually completed in one year. Whereas the sculptures which were to decorate the building, the construction of the aviary by Girolamo Rainaldi (1617-1619) and the landscaping of the garden took until circa 1620.

As early as 1627, a copy of the plan of the building was published in a treatise on civic archiecture, by Joseph Furttenbach, an architect from Augusta, who described it as follows: "In the Borghese Garden outside the city it is good to see the small palace built by the talented architect Giovanni van Santen (Vasanzio), in which I found such intelligence displayed in the arrangement and good proportions of the rooms, that I should like to draw up a plan for those who appreciate civic architecture, so that they can see what this design is like [...] it aims at the following effect: firstly that the appearance of the building be noble, courageous, strong and well contained; secondly that the pilasters be equidistant from one another to give the stone façade an heroic aspect [...]; thirdly that the windows and doors be in perfect harmony and that, wherever one is in the palace, one may see the entire building in perspective and one may have fresh air, which is not only beneficial to man, but also most beneficial and necessary for the whole building [...] a charming, ornamental, spiral staircase sculpted in white marble leads to the upper rooms, where there are many fine paintings [..] the aforementioned palace has been built solely of brick, left white on the surface and decorated with projecting cornices. However, many antique sculptures have been set in the wall betwen the framed windows and pilasters. Close by is a very beautiful garden, with an aviary and fountains: one can therefore say that it has a beautiful aspect worthy of a prince."

Apart from the contribution made by the Flemish architect Vasanzio, the architectural features described here are to be attributed above all to Flaminio Ponzio, an extraordinary architect in whom the Pope and the Cardinal placed absolute trust. Ponzio designed the proportions of the rooms, and the Doric order on the exterior. He freed its architecture from the traditional style of other villas, which was more monolithic and confined, causing unexpected front and side projections to emerge in a dynamic relationship with the upward movement of the towers, which is enhanced by the arrangement of the windows and the doors commu-

Porphyry Bath, 2nd-3rd cent. AD

nicating with the garden avenues on all four sides. Vasanzio succeeded Ponzio after his death in 1613. A cabinet-maker by training, he was responsible for the elaborate embellishment of the façades, with their ornate reliefs and stuccoes, for the interior decoration, fountains and gardens; the latter were also the work of Domenico Savino da Montepulciano.

The history of the sculpture and painting collections

The original sculptures and paintings in the Borghese Gallery date back to Cardinal Scipione's collection, though subsequent events over the next three centuries entailing both losses and acquisitions have left their mark.

Cardinal Scipione was drawn to any

D. Dossi, *Circe* or *Melissa*, c.1520

works of ancient, Renaissance and contemporary art which might re-evoke a new golden age. He was not particularly interested in medieval art, but passionately sought to acquire antique sculpture and, if it was fragmentary, had it restored by such brilliant sculptors as Pietro and Gian Lorenzo Bernini (see Entrance Hall) or Nicolas Cordier (see Room X).

A large number of these ancient marbles that came to light during construction work in Rome (see the *Battle Relief* from St. Peter's, now in the portico) were papal gifts, and hence undeniably the personal property of Cardinal Scipione. In 1607, he bought some important sculptures from Tiberio Ceoli's collection, formerly in Palazzo Sacchetti, including the monumental *Fighting Satyr* and the *Dionysus* (now in the Entrance Hall). Thanks to the Pope's brothers, Giambattista and Francesco, and his nephew the Cardinal, in 1609, the famous collection of sculptures from Tommaso della Porta's bequest was added to that of the Borghese family. These included the outstanding ancient *Centaur Tamed by Cupid* (now in the Louvre) and the busts of the *Twelve Emperors* by Giovan Battista della Porta (set in the upper ovals in the Entrance Hall).

But Cardinal Scipione was so ambitious that he promoted the creation of new sculptures and especially marble groups to rival antique works; a challenge brilliantly met by Gian Lorenzo Bernini, Nicolas Cordier and Antonio Susini. During the 17th century sculptures by Alessandro Algardi (*Sleep*) and François Duquesnoy (*Bacchanalia of Putti*, Room VI) also entered the collection.

Few of the brilliant works executed by Luigi Valadier in the 18th century have come down to us, but the *Herm of Bacchus* (Room 1) is a significant example. The statue of *Pauline Bonaparte*, executed by Canova between 1805 and 1808, has been in the villa since 1838. In 1807, Camillo Borghese sold Napoleon 154 statues, 160 busts, 170 bas-reliefs, 30 columns and various vases, which constitute the 'Borghese Collection' in the Louvre. But already by the 1830s these gaps seem to have been filled by new finds from recent excavations and works recuperated from the cellars and various other Borghese residences. These were installed for Prince Camillo by his minister Evasio Gozzani and by the architect Luigi Canina.

In the 20th century, the sculpture collection was enriched by Bernini's *Truth* (1924) and his terracotta model for the *Equestrian Statue of Louis XIV* (donated by Count A. Contini Bonacossi), Giuliano Finelli's *Bust of Cardinal Domenico Ginnasi*, Pietro Bracci's *Bust of Clement XII*, the important 1768 stucco model of *Saint John the Baptist* in the act of baptizing by Giovanni Antonio Houdon (in the Chapel), as well as a 16th-century *Bust of Christ* (in the Entrance Hall), which was controversially attributed to Michelangelo in 1984.

Cardinal Scipione's collection of paintings was remarkable and was poetically described as early as 1613 by Scipione Francucci. In 1607, the Pope gave the Cardinal 107 paintings which had been confiscated from the painter Giuseppe Cesari, called the Cavalier d'Arpino. In the following year, Raphael's *Deposition* was secretly removed from the Baglioni Chapel in the church of S. Francesco in Perugia and transported to Rome. It was given to Cardinal Scipione through a papal *motu proprio*. In 1616-1617, Domenichino spent some days in prison for having refused to deliver the so-called *Diana* to Cardinal Scipione Borghese (the painting had been commissioned by another cardinal, Pietro Aldobrandini). In 1608, through the good offices of Cardinal G. Bentivoglio, some paintings from the Ferrara School were acquired, including works by Dosso Dossi. The inventory that would enable us to identify the large group of paintings purchased from Cardinal Emilio Sfondrato in the same year is lost. Cardinal Scipione also personally commissioned many paintings from Caravaggio, Rubens, Lanfranco, Guercino, Guido Reni, Gianfrancesco Guerrieri, Claudio Deruet and Lavinia Fontana, as well as the miniature mosaics by Marcello Provenzale. In 1682, part of Olimpia Aldobrandini's inheritance entered the Borghese collection; it included works from the collections of Cardinal Salviati and Lucrezia d'Este. Many of the 18th-century paintings that originally decorated the villa have been lost, including the large landscapes by Hackert for Room XIV, the animal paintings by Wenzel Peter and three large canvases

J. Bruegel the Elder, attrib. to, *Flowers*, beginning of the 17th cent.

by Gavin Hamilton that completed the decoration of the Helen and Paris Room (Room XIX), today in Palazzo Braschi, Rome. Various paintings were given to the Borghese Gallery by the sculptor B. Cavaceppi. In 1818, Camillo Borghese bought the magnificent canvas by Sassoferrato, which reinterprets the Mackintosh *Madonna* by Raphael, as well as Guercino's *Prodigal Son*, Carlo Dolci's *Madonna of the Finger* and the *Martyrdom of St. Gennaro*, attributed to Fracanzano. In 1827, Prince Camillo also bought Correggio's celebrated *Danäe* in Paris.

In 1919, Baron von Messinger donated the pair of portraits by Gaspare Landi (his *Self-Portrait* and his *Portrait of Antonio Canova*) and, in 1911, he also gave Bernini's *Self-Portrait* as a middle-aged man to the collection. Two further portraits by Bernini were purchased in 1919. The most recent acquisition is the *Portrait of the Duke of Alba* by an unknown artist purchased in 1987.

Past and present criteria for exhibiting artworks

Today's display of the works is very different from their original arrangement under Scipione Borghese described in detail by G. Manilli (1650). In fact, after the Cardinal's death in 1633 no major changes were made until 1650. Originally the works were not arranged systematically according to medium adopted, artist or theme. Sacred subjects were hung next to secular ones, landscapes next to still lifes, large pictures above smaller ones. However, there were occasional groups of paintings on the same theme which allowed comparisons to be made. For example, the Entrance Hall, where Caravaggio's *Madonna of the Palafrenieri* was to be found, also contained three large pictures depicting *Adam and Eve* by the Cavalier d'Arpino, Baglione and Passignano respectively; in Room II one could compare the large *Venus* by Cranach with that by Brescianino; Room III housed the *Cain Killing Abel* by one of Annibale Carracci's pupils and the *David Killing Goliath* by Giulio Romano; Room IV was devoted to "portraits of Potentates and great Princes" including Rudolf II, Sigismund III, Anne of Spain, Archdukes Matthew and Albert of Austria, Pope Paul V, his father Marcantonio and various members of the Borghese family. In what is now Room VIII, however, an initial attempt was made to group the pictures according to artistic criteria. Caravaggio's *Supper at Emmaus* (now in the National Gallery, London) was flanked by Jacopo Bassano's *Last Supper*, which was accompanied by a series of twelve other paintings by the Bassano family (it is known that Caravaggio had shown an interest in the "humble" art of the Bassanos). Walnut stools were frequently used as supports for the statues and small sculptures were set on tall precious columns like idols.

In the 18th-century rearrangement of the collection particular care was taken to harmonize the interior decoration of the rooms with the paintings. After the sculptures were sold to Napoleon, the alterations made by Asprucci and, later, especially by Canina, focussed on symmetry in the arrangement of ancient reliefs which were carved into pieces and decoratively set in the walls and on the front of the bases supporting the statues. In this period the ground floor was reserved for statues, while paintings were housed on the first floor. This trend reflected the new concepts of museum design found in the Museo Pio Clementino and the Musée Napoléon in Paris, to which Ennio Quirino Visconti contributed. He also compiled the essential catalogue of the ancient statues in Villa Borghese. The organization of the museum was conceived as an ascent from the more ancient pieces (the sculptures on the ground floor) towards more sublime forms of art such as the paintings on the *piano nobile*, which were placed in rooms that were more suitable from the climatic and conservation point of view. In 1891, when the collection of paintings from the palazzo at Ripetta was transferred to Villa Borghese, A. Venturi and G. Cantalamessa arranged the works in chronological order according to schools of painting, a policy that has never been entirely free of inconsistencies, but which was substantially followed in the subsequent arrangement by Paola della Pergola.

A new arrangement of the paintings became necessary in order to reopen large windows that had been blocked up (Rooms X and XX). This was organized according to the following criteria: given that for security reasons only a limited number of visitors can enter the picture-gallery, major works had also to be displayed on the ground floor. The paintings have been arranged to reflect the themes of the central statues. Thus the thematic link between the central sculptures and ceiling paintings also extends to the walls, as envisioned in the 18th-century arrangement. Room VIII is devoted to Caravaggio and the painters inspired by him, as well as to his teacher the Cavalier d'Arpino.

On the first floor the paintings are arranged chronologically by school, but this is restricted to the individual rooms. This choice was made in order to respect the extraordinary 18th-century architecture of the villa's interior. Thus superimposed oblong shapes no longer cut the wall pilasters in half and a huge painting like Lanfranco's *Norandino* no longer takes up the small chapel so it is now possible to view it in its entirety. For conservation reasons paintings are no longer hung near the windows.

[1] "I, custodian of Villa Borghese, publicly declare as follows: Whoever you may be, provided you are a free man, do not fear the hindrance of regulations; go where you will, ask what you desire; leave when you wish. These delights have been created more for visitors than for the owner. In the golden century in which security renders everything gold, the owner forbids strict laws to be imposed on the visitor who lingers here. May the friend find good will here in place of the law, if on the contrary someone with deliberate and conscious evil intent, breaks the golden law of courtesy, be warned that the custodian will tear up his card of friendship." See B di Gaddo, *Villa Borghese, il Giardino e le Architetture*, Rome, 1985, p.58.

[2] The restoration of the double staircase was exceuted by the Soprintendenza per i Beni Ambientali e Architettonici, under the guidance of F. Zurli and G. Palandri. This affords access to the lower ground level housing various amenities that was formerly the kitchen and storerooms, whereas the circular room was used for storing water.

The Borghese Gallery

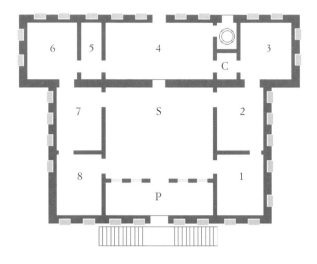

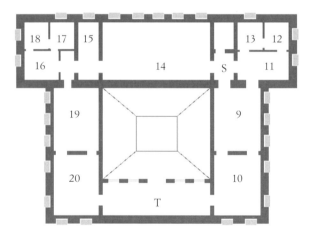

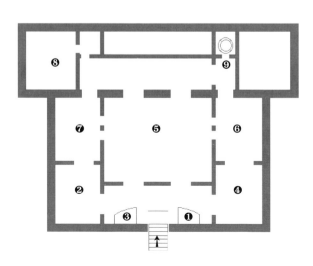

GROUND FLOOR

P   Portico
S   Entrance Hall
C   Chapel

ROOMS

1   Pauline
2   David
3   Apollo and Daphne
4   The Emperors
5   Hermaphrodite
6   Aeneas and Anchises
7   Egyptian
8   Faun

FIRST FLOOR Picture Gallery

T   Terrace
S   Entrance Hall
9   Florentine School, 16th cent.
10 Italian Mannerism, 16th cent.
11 Ferrara School, 16th cent.
12 Siena, Lombardy and Veneto
    Schools, 16th cent.
13 Florentine School, 16th cent.
14 Gallery of Lanfranco,
    17th-cent. painting
15 Ferrara, Veneto and Brescia
    Schools, 16th cent.
16 Florentine Mannerism,
    16th cent.
17 17th- and 18th-cent. painting
18 17th-cent. painting
19 17th-cent. painting in Rome
20 Veneto School, 16th cent.

Lower Ground Level - Services and Amenities

→   Entrance
❶   Tickets and information
❷   Bookshop
❸   Audio-guides and cloakroom
❹   Exhibition Hall
❺   Lecture and Multimedia Hall
❻   Educational area
❼   Bar and Restaurant
❽   Toilets
❾   Lifts and Stairs

Façade and portico

In contrast with its appearance in 1984, the glowing façade of the villa set in its green garden, has now been returned to its original 17th-century splendour, depicted in the picture by J. W. Baur, 1636. The façade's creamy marble colour and paler background tones have been restored and the pilaster strips and string-courses are a shade of ivory resembling travertine. The colour, the Doric order of pilasters and the harmonious proportions of the whole building are reminiscent of classical architecture. The original double staircase by F. Ponzio has been reconstructed and will be surmounted by a copy of an ancient vase with two cornucopias (the originals are in the Louvre). This replaces the late 18th-century pyramid-shaped staircase and now provides access to the lower ground level containing various amenities. The shutters that altered the original design of the windows have recently been removed. All the busts and statues on the façade, which had sadly deteriorated owing to lack of routine maintenance and were eroded by rain, wind, dust and lichen, have now been restored. These include a striking *Antique Hercules*, a copy of the original by Lysippus from the collection of Francesco Piccolomini, later Pope Pius III. Recent restoration work has saved this statue, which originally stood on the terrace. Its legs had become extremely fragile since rust on the support pins had fragmented the ankles and one of the feet into more than forty

PALATII VILLAE BVRGHESIAE PROSPECTVS

J. W. Baur, *View of Villa Borghese*, 1636

Villa Borghese, façade after restoration in 1997

pieces, which have now been recomposed. The head of Marcus Aurelius as a young man, designed and executed by the sculptor Giuseppe Ducrot (1996), has been added to a formerly headless 17th-century bust of mediocre quality in the last of the oval niches on the façade. The portico, which was open until grilles were added in the 19th century, houses some outstanding ancient sculptures and reliefs that have now been restored. The three large friezes depicting scenes from the Emperor Trajan's victory over the Dacians in 106 AD (two of which have been set in the shorter walls of the portico) and the splendid sarcophagus with scenes of the battle between the Romans and the barbarians, dating from circa 205 AD, underline a theme already present on the façade, and on those of many 16th-century Roman palazzi. Colossal statues of Dacian prisoners formerly flanked the staircase. These were ancient porphyry sculptures with additions by Pietro Bernini (now in the Louvre). Two 16th-century reliefs based on famous drawings by Michelangelo are also set high up in the portico. They depict *Prometheus Bound*, with an eagle eating his liver, and *Leda and the Swan*. A particularly fine Greek bust of *Narcissus*, attributed to the school of Polycletus, stands on a column of *lumachella*, to the right as you enter. After the losses in Napoleonic times, Luigi Canina rearranged the portico and the other rooms containing sculptures.

THE CAPITOLINE GEESE

THE RIVER TIBER

THE ERITREAN SIBYL

MAEAN YL

NDER AND EIT

JOY WITH GRAPES

SPIRIT OF AMOR PATRIAE WITH CROWN

REMUS WITH THE HELMET OF HIS FATHER MARS

FAME AND HISTORY

TH UNVEILED

TIME

JUPITER

ROME TRIUMPHANT

JUSTICE FIDELITY HONOUR

ROMULUS

ROMAN VICTORY AND MARS

ROMULUS WITH THE SHE-WOLF

SITY

SPIRIT OF ROMAN VICTORY WITH PALM

FURIUS CAMILLUS IN THE BATTLE AGAINST THE GAULS

MAEAN YL

BRENNUS DEFEATED

TIBURTINE SIBYL

Fresco on the ceiling and chiaroscuro paintings on the walls: Mariano Rossi, 1775-1778
Chiaroscuro medallions above the windows: Gioacchino Agricola
Animals and pilaster decorations: Wenzel Peter
Imitation cameo reliefs: A. Brunetti, F. Carradori, M. Laboureur, F. Monti, V. Pacetti, T. Righi, L. Salimei
Allegories and puttis above the niches: Agostino Penna

Above: Marcus Curtius (Hellenistic horse, 1st-2nd cent. AD, Curtius by Pietro Bernini, c.1618, restored by A. Penna in 1776) / 2 Colossal statues, 2nd cent. AD, in the niches: Fighting Satyr, copy of an original from Taranto, with head added by Pietro and Gian Lorenzo Bernini, and statue of Bacchus, copy of a Praxiteles original / on the respective bases: sections of a relief with scenes of the cult of Dionysus 1st cent. AD no. VIIII / 4 Colossal heads: Emperors Hadrian (c.135 AD) and Antoninus Pius (160 AD), Divinity restored as Isis with a lotus flower (c.160 AD) and Juno (1st cent. AD) / Portrait of Augustus as Pontifex Maximus (10-70 AD) / Funerary monument to Petronia Musa, Greek poetess, framed in a seashell (120 AD) / in the window niches: Head of Christ, formerly attrib. to Michelangelo (16th cent.) / 2 Monumental candlesticks composed of antique and 18th-cent. pieces / Group of Mars, Venus and Cupid (c.150 AD) / in the upper niches: busts of the twelve Caesars by Giov. Batt. della Porta (before 1597) no. LIII / Mosaic pavement with gladiators (320 AD) from Torrenova on the Via Casilina.

Marcus Curtius Flinging himself into the Chasm, 1st- 2nd cent. AD (statue of Curtius by P. Bernini)

This imposing hall welcomes the visitor to the villa with a celebration of the glory of Roman civilization. The fresco on the ceiling depicts the *Apotheosis of Romulus* received in Olympus by Jupiter, while propitiating the victory of the Roman hero Furius Camillus over the Gauls, led by Brennus. This auspicious subject was chosen to celebrate the birth of Marcantonio IV Borghese's first son (8 August 1775) and brilliantly painted with late Baroque panache by the Sicilian artist Mariano Rossi, between 1775 and 1778. 19th-century overpainting, which weighed down the cornice and created an ochre barrier between the ceiling and the walls, could still be seen in March 1997. Restoration has now revealed the original delicate gilding on the horizontal portions of the cornice, which alternate with fake marble decorations reflecting the colour of the ceiling and the walls. The walls are divided into classical-style panels with plant, bird and animal motifs, painted by Wenzel Peter and feature stuccoes and cameos, executed by sculptors V. Pacetti, F. Carradori, M. Laboureur, T. Righi, L. Salimei and A. Brunetti. Recent restoration has revealed that the background of the cameos consisted of delicate shades of light blue, sea green, warm beige and pink. A large equestrian statue of the hero *Marcus Curtius* sacrificing himself for his people by flinging himself into the chasm of the Roman Forum is set high up on the wall. At the time of Cardinal Scipione, the exceptionally fine ancient sculpture of the horse in Pentelicus marble had been restored with the addition of the statue of Marcus Curtius by Pietro Bernini, and stood outside the villa in the vicinity of the

Bacchus, 2nd cent. AD

Fighting Satyr, 120-140 AD

Mosaic with Gladiators, 320 AD

orange grove (towards Via Pinciana). Four ancient colossal heads enhance the magnificence of this hall: the emperors Hadrian (c.135 AD) and Antoninus Pius with, opposite, a female head from the Antonine Age (c.160-180 AD), restored to represent an Isis by adding a lotus flower, and finally a Juno (1st century AD). These are flanked by niches containing two remarkable ancient sculptures from the Ceoli Collection, a *Bacchus* highly reminiscent of Praxiteles and a *Satyr*, in a twisting pose raising a *pedum* or shepherd's crook in a threatening or joking gesture. This is a marble copy of a Hellenistic bronze original from Taranto. Recent restoration has removed the thick encrustations from the torso and head, caused by its exposure to the elements, and confirmed the hypothesis put forward by archaeologist P. Moreno that the head had been restored by Pietro and Gian Lorenzo Bernini. This attacking satyr also inspired the pose of Gian Lorenzo Bernini's *David.* Below the *Satyr* and the *Bacchus* are fragments of a Neo-Attic relief dating from the 1st century BC depicting scenes from the cult of Bacchus. Other pieces of this valuable relief were removed and used to decorate the walls of the Villa Borghese in the Neoclassical period (in the Entrance Hall above the door leading to Room IV and in Room II, above the relief depicting scenes from the life of Hercules). The delicate monument to the Greek poetess, Petronia Musa, dating from around 120 AD, shows the deceased in an elegant sea shell.

Bizarre candelsticks consisting of various ancient pieces and 18th-century additions reflect the taste that was to influence Piranesi's drawings. The famous 4th-century AD mosaic depicting gladiators fighting was found on the Borghese estate of Torre Nova on the Via Casilina and set in the floor of the Entrance Hall in the 19th century. Whoever was responsible for blocking the entrance to the Room of the Emperors with these mosaics failed to understand the importance of the villa's central axis that passed directly from the fountain at the centre of the forecourt in front of the façade through the portico, the Entrance Hall and Room IV.

Room I
Formerly called the Room of the Vase (now in the Louvre)

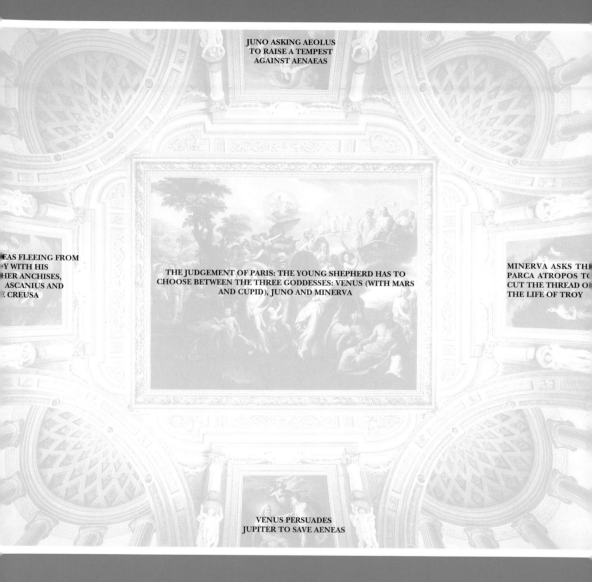

JUNO ASKING AEOLUS
TO RAISE A TEMPEST
AGAINST AENAEAS

EAS FLEEING FROM
Y WITH HIS
HER ANCHISES,
ASCANIUS AND
E CREUSA

THE JUDGEMENT OF PARIS: THE YOUNG SHEPHERD HAS TO
CHOOSE BETWEEN THE THREE GODDESSES: VENUS (WITH MARS
AND CUPID), JUNO AND MINERVA

MINERVA ASKS TH
PARCA ATROPOS TO
CUT THE THREAD O
THE LIFE OF TROY

VENUS PERSUADES
JUPITER TO SAVE AENEAS

Pictures transferred to the ceiling: Domenico de Angelis, 1779
Illusionist decorations: Giovanni Battista Marchetti

Sculptures: A. Canova, Pauline Bonaparte, 1805-08, no. LIV / L. Valadier, Herm of Bacchus, 1773, no. LXVII / Portrait in grey marble of Bassianus, father of the Empress Julia Domna, 195 AD , no. LXVII / P. Bracci, Portrait of Pope Clement XII, c.1735, no. CCLXXII / Square reliefs: Ajax and Cassandra, 370 AD, no. LXIV / Minos' Sacrifice to Poseidon, 1st cent. AD, no. LXXIV / Cupid on an Eagle, attrib. to P. Bernini, c. 1618 / 2 Rectangular reliefs by V. Pacetti: Mercury considers the fates of Hector and Achilles and Achilles learns of the death of Patroclus / Sarcophagus with columns depicting Apollo and the Muses, c. 220 AD, no. LXXV / Bust, 140 AD, restored in the 16th cent. as Isis with Borgia heraldic relief, no. LXC / in the corners: 4 hooded genies, no. LXV-LXIX / Groups: Leda and the Swan and Venus and Cupid bathing, no. LXXII: 18th-cent. caprice composition with 2nd cent. AD elements.

Antonio Canova, *Pauline Bonaparte*, 1805-1808

The reclining *Pauline Bonaparte* in the center of the room holds an apple in her hand evoking the *Venus Victrix* in the judgement of Paris, who was chosen to settle a dispute between Juno (power), Minerva (arts and sciences) and Venus (love). The same subject was painted on the ceiling by Domenico de Angelis (1779), framed by Giovan Battista Marchetti's tromp d'oeil architecture, and was inspired by a famous relief on the façade of the Villa Medici. This marble statue of Pauline in a highly refined pose is considered a supreme example of the Neoclassical style. Antonio Canova executed this sculpture between 1805 ans 1808 without the customary drapery of a person of high rank, an exception at the time, thus transforming this historical figure into a goddess of antiquity in a pose of classical tranquillity and noble simplicity. The wooden base, draped like a catafalque, once contained a mechanism that caused the sculpture to rotate, as in the case of other works by Canova. The roles of artwork and spectator were thus reversed, it was the sculpture that moved whilst the spectator stood still and observed the splendid statue from all angles. In the past, viewers admired the softly gleaming sculpture of Pauline by candlelight and its lustre was not only due to the fine quality of the marble but also to the waxed surface, which has been recently restored. Opposite the statue of Pauline stands an extraordinary work by the sculptor Luigi Valadier, the *Herm of Bacchus* (1773). This refined bronze head has been patinated in green copper tones by the artist and crowned with a wreath of gilded ivy leaves. Four ancient circular altars serve as bases for statues;

Luigi Valadier, *Herm of Bacchus*, 1773

Furious Ajax and Cassandra, 370 BC

one of these altars decorated with *bucra-nia*, or ox-head motifs, and garlands, reworked in the 17th century, formerly supported Bernini's *Aeneas and Anchises* (Room VI). This was far lower than the bases used for Bernini's works in the Borghese Gallery between the 18th and 20th centuries. The two sides of a fine sarcophagus decorated with small columns and depicting Apollo and the Muses are set high up on the walls. They illustrate the art of drilling and fret-work ornamentation common in Asia Minor in the first half of the 1st century AD. The sarcophagus was sawn in two so that it could be displayed symmetrically. One of the four square reliefs dramatically depicts a *Furious Ajax*, snatching Cassandra, daughter of the king of Troy, from the altar of the temple of Athena. This relief of very fine workmanship was executed around 370 BC by a sculptor from Taranto. On the opposite wall, another square relief illustrates the strength of *Cupid Taming Jupiter's Eagle* (reminiscent of the eagle on the Borghese coat of arms), a work executed in the antique style by Pietro Bernini. The four corners contain four small Roman genies, the forerunners of modern gnomes, which were considered either good or bad omens in antiquity.

Room II
Called the Room of the Sun

APOLLO RIDING IN
HIS CHARIOT

JUPITER FULMINATES PHAETON WHO IS
INCAPABLE OF DRIVING THE CHARIOT
OF THE SUN

...SPER HOLDING
...RCHES TOWARDS
...E DARKENED
...RTH

DARKNESS COVERS THE
EARTH AS A PUTTO
CARRIES THE STAR OF
VENUS

THE HELIADES MOURN
THE FALL OF PHAETON

Central painting: Francesco Caccianiga, 1775-1777
Medallions, nudes, putti: Gioacchino Agricola
Illusionist decorations: Giovanni Battista Marchetti

Sculptures: G. L. Bernini, David, 1623-24, no. LXXVII / Sarcophagus with the Labours of Hercules on two sides, 160 AD, no. LXXIX / above: relief with scenes of the cult of Dionysus, 1st cent. AD, inv. IIIC, and sarcophagus with a marine Thiasus and a deceased as Venus in the seashell, 220 AD, no. LXXXI / Relief: copy of the figure of the Sun and his chariot, formerly in the Capitoline Temple of Jupiter, Oceanus, Moon on the descending chariot, no. LXXXIX / Portrait of a sovereign as Alexander the Great, 221-4 AD, on an altar with a deer, 1st cent. AD, no. VIIC / Capitoline-style Aphrodite, 1st cent. AD, no. C / Statue of Dionysus restored as Apollo, 1st cent. AD, no. CCXXXXI / Colossal head of Hercules, 150 AD, no. LXXXIII.
Paintings: R. Manetti, Andromeda, no. 4 / B. Caracciolo, David with the Head of Goliath, dated 1612, no. 2 / Annibale Carracci, Samson in Prison, c.1595, no. 23 / Caravaggiesque painter, Still Life with Birds and Still Life with Lizards, 1602-1607, nos. 301, 54.

It was Cardinal Scipione Borghese who commissioned the statue of *David*, confronting the giant Goliath and armed only with a sling, executed between 1623 and 1624 by twenty-five-year-old Gian Lorenzo Bernini. The youth's tense facial expression is modelled on Bernini himself as he struggled with his tools to work the hard marble. The oversize cuirass leant to David by King Saul before the encounter lies on the ground with the harp David will play after his victory, which is decorated with an eagle's head, a symbolic reference to the Borghese family. The number of points of view the sculptor intended to present to the spectator is still a matter of conjecture. The right side shows David's movements, his stride is almost a leap as he aims his sling; seen from the front the pose is frozen, just one second before the fatal shot, and seen diagonally there is a rhythmic balance between movement and pose.

The painting on the wall behind by Battistello Carracciolo (1612) depicts the same subject. Here in Caravaggiesque shadows, David appears triumphant beside the giant's decapitated head, wearing a fashionable jaunty red hat with long plumes. The *Samson in Prison* (c.1595), a painting in the heroic style by Annibale Carracci, pays a tribute to the 'prisons' of Michelangelo and the vibrant colours and broad brush-strokes of Titian's later works. The large painting by the Sienese artist Rutilio Manetti, *Perseus Freeing Andromeda from the Sea Monster*, also reflects Titian's influence on Baroque painting at the beginning of the 17th century. The front panels of splendid ancient sarcophagi that were added to the interior decorations of the room at the beginning of the 19th century, include the striking scenes of the labours of Hercules, executed in Asia Minor around 160 AD, framed by oriental arches on small columns. The bust of Alexander the Great, with an inspired expression, is a good Roman copy of an original by Lysippus. Francesco Caccianiga executed the central painting on the ceiling between 1775 and 1777. It depicts the *Fall of Phaethon*, reckless son of the Sun-Apollo, struck down by Jupiter for having lost control of the chariot of the Sun and causing havoc in heaven and on earth. Gioacchino Agricola added amusing putti playing games and mythological medallions to the elegant ceiling, which was divided into panels by Giovan Battista Marchetti's illusionist painting.

G. L. Bernini, *David*, 1623-1624

G. L. Bernini, *David*, detail, 1623-1624

Room III
Room of Apollo and Daphne

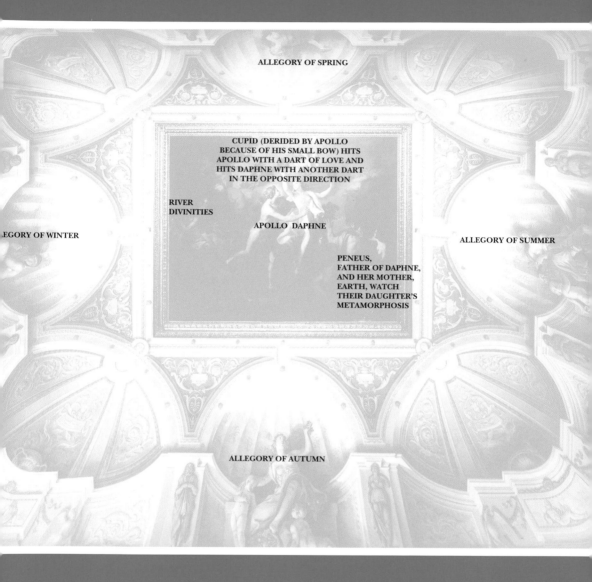

ALLEGORY OF SPRING

CUPID (DERIDED BY APOLLO
BECAUSE OF HIS SMALL BOW) HITS
APOLLO WITH A DART OF LOVE AND
HITS DAPHNE WITH ANOTHER DART
IN THE OPPOSITE DIRECTION

RIVER
DIVINITIES

APOLLO DAPHNE

EGORY OF WINTER

ALLEGORY OF SUMMER

PENEUS,
FATHER OF DAPHNE,
AND HER MOTHER,
EARTH, WATCH
THEIR DAUGHTER'S
METAMORPHOSIS

ALLEGORY OF AUTUMN

Central painting and four seasons in chiaroscuro: Pietro Angeletti, 1780-85
Illusionist decorations: Giovanni Battista Marchetti

Sculptures: G. L. Bernini, Apollo and Daphne, 1622-1625, no. CV / Boys with ducks, 2nd cent. AD, on triangular bases one of which is antique, 130 AD, and the other an 18th-cent. copy by A. Penna, no. CVI-CX / Statue of a woman restored as Isis, 2nd cent. AD, no. CXI / Group of a Fountain and Fisherman, c.210 AD, no. CVII / Candlestick with Hermes, Dionysus and Aphrodite, 1st cent. AD, on a base with a dance scene, c.75 BC, no. CXVI / Alabaster lion, 2nd cent. AD, restored in the 18th. cent., no. CXXXXII / between the columns: Statue of Apollo with Griffin and Tripod and opposite, Medici-style Venus with Dolphin and Cupid, no. CVIII / Colossal head of Apollo, all 2nd cent. AD, no. CXX.
Paintings: Dosso Dossi, Apollo and Daphne, c.1522, no. 1 / Paul Brill and assistant, Fantastic Landscapes, c.1595, nos. 13 and 18 / Dosso Dossi, Giovanni Luteri, Circe or Melissa, c.1520, no. 217.

G. L. Bernini, *Apollo and Daphne*, 1622-1625

Gian Lorenzo Bernini created an unprecedented masterpiece for Cardinal Scipione Borghese depicting the chaste nymph Daphne being turned into a laurel tree, pursued in vain by Apollo god of light. This life-size marble sculpture, begun by Bernini at the age of twenty-four and executed between 1622 and 1625, has always been housed in the same room in the villa, but origi-nally stood on a lower and nar-rower base set against the wall near the stairs. Consequently anyone enter-ing the room first saw Apollo from behind, then the fleeing n y m p h appeared in the process of meta-morphosis. Bark covers most of her body, but according to Ovid's lines, Apollo's hand can still feel her heart beating beneath it. Thus the scene ends by Daphne being transformed into a laurel tree to escape her divine aggressor. The presence of this pagan myth in the Car-dinal's villa was justified by a moral cou-plet composed in Latin by Cardinal Maf-feo Barberini (later Pope Urban VIII) and engraved on the cartouche on the base, which says: *Those who love to pursue*

D. Dossi, *Apollo and Daphne*, detail, c.1522

fleeting forms of pleasure, in the end find only leaves and bitter berries in their hands. In 1785, when Marcantonio IV Borghese decided to place the work in the centre of the room, Vincenzo Pacetti designed the present base by using the original pieces, adding plaster to the plinth and another cartouche bearing the Borghese eagle, sculpted by Lorenzo Cardelli. In 1780, Pietro Angeletti took up the theme of the sculpture in the illusionistic painting on the ceiling and also painted the four seasons in chiaroscuro framed by the trompe l'oeil architectural motifs brilliant-ly executed by Giovan Battista Marchetti. The theme of meta-morphosis is also depicted in the two famous pictures by Dosso Dossi, the beautiful *Circe* or *Melissa* (c.1530), who changes human beings into lemurs on the nearby tree and *Apol-lo* (1524) (the body of Apollo is reminis-cent of the ancient *Apollo Belevedere*, now in the Vatican Museums). The god of light and poetry, wearing a laurel wreath, sadly plays eternal melodies after losing Daphne, who appears as a small figure in the background.

G. Agricola, *Worshipping Angels*, c.1780

The only place where wall paintings dating from Cardinal Scipione's time can still be seen is the chapel. Here recent restoration work has been carried out on *The Assumption* by C. Deruet (1617-1618), depicting God the Father above, flanked by Carlo Borromeo and Francesca Romana, who were canonized by Pope Paul V. There is also a *John the Baptist* (1767-1768) baptizing, a plaster model for a sculpture by Giovanni Antonio Houdon that is in the church of S. Maria degli Angeli. The figure is an exact anatomical study based on the so-called 'écorché' (skinned model) in the Villa Medici, used for training artists. The chapel is decorated with two small 16th century valuable altars. The altar in silver and ebony, dating from around the end of the 16th century, is an example of very fine craftsmanship by Matthias Wallbaum, a goldsmith from Augusta. The other altar by Guiglielmo della Porta has a *Calvary* in wax on slate in the central panel (c.1565), probably a preliminary sketch for one of the scenes on a bronze door for St Peter's, which was never exceuted, while the frame of ebony and semi-precious stones dates from the beginning of the 17th century. The large canvas depicting the *Pietà of the Angels* by Federico Zuccari (c.1567) is a copy of a much-admired painting by his brother Taddeo (1560-1566) (formerly in the Vitelleschi Collection, now in a private collection) executed on a panel for the chapel in the Palazzo Farnese at Caprarola.

Room IV
Called the Gallery or Room of the Emperors

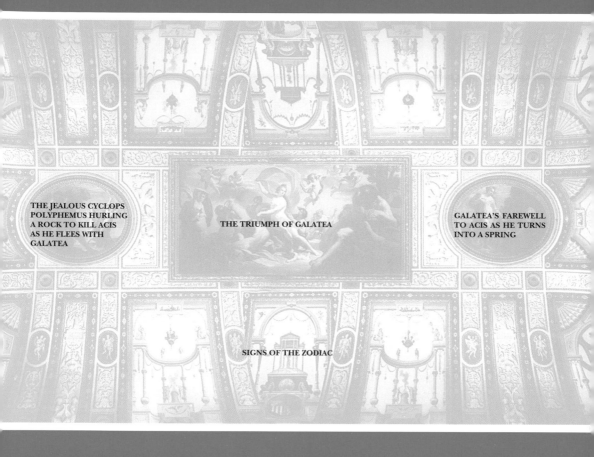

THE JEALOUS CYCLOPS POLYPHEMUS HURLING A ROCK TO KILL ACIS AS HE FLEES WITH GALATEA

THE TRIUMPH OF GALATEA

GALATEA'S FAREWELL TO ACIS AS HE TURNS INTO A SPRING

SIGNS OF THE ZODIAC

Large pictures transferred to the ceiling: Domenico de Angelis, 1778-1780
Small medallions and pictures: Gioacchino Agricola
Illusionist decorations and landscapes with ruins: Giovanni Battitsa Marchetti

Sculptures: G.L. Bernini, Pluto and Proserpina, 1621-22, no. CCLXVIII / Bronze figure of Neptune by G. L. Bernini, c.1628, and the Farnese Bull by A. Susini, 1613, no. CCXLIX / 4 Cantharus-shaped vases with representations of the seasons by M. Laboureur and L. Cardelli, 1785 / niches in the long wall: Diana restored as a Muse with a mask, another Diana, a statue of Bacchus, 1st-3rd cent. AD and the Borghese Artemis, 4th cent. BC, nos. CXXVI-CXXIX-CXXXIV-CXXXVII / niches in the short walls: Cloaked Venus, 1st cent. BC, and Bacchus with a Panther, 2nd cent. AD, no. CXXXXIII / 17 Porphyry busts of Emperors and one of Juno by an unknown artist, respectively early 17th and late 18th cent., nos. CXXXVI-CXXXXVIII-CXXXV-CXXXIX-CLXII-CLVII-CXXVIII-CXXXXIX-CXXVII-CLII-CLVIII-CXL-CLV-CLI-CXXXXIV-CLIV-CXXIV / 2 Porphyry tables with heads of the four seasons by L. Valadier, 1773 /2 Porphyry goblets, one antique and the other by Paolo Santi, 1783.

The Borghese Artemis, 4th cent. BC

This room was also designed by the architect Antonio Asprucci, whose late 18th-century project for the interior of the villa harmonized proportions and colours, avoiding Baroque ostentation and Neoclassical severity. This harmonious design begins with the precious marble pavement, continues in the rhythmic order of the columns and culminates in the ribbon motifs dividing up the ceiling. Valuable antique sculptures are set in the gilded niches and these include the *Borghese Artemis* (near the door leading to Room V), a rare original by a Greek master from the 4th century BC. Refined mosaics and grotesques by Cesare Aguatti are resplendent between the columns (these are decorations inspired by those in the grottoes of antiquity).

These airy grotesques with their tall, slim columns and the addition of Roman views on the ceiling reflect not so much Renaissance art as that of ancient Rome. At the time, the sensational rediscovery of the ancient Villa Negroni (1777) had provided a wide range of examples of this art. In the paintings on the ceiling Domenico de Angelis depicted the *Story and Triumph of Galatea* (1778-1780), a sea nymph who preferred the young Acis to the Cyclops Polyphemus, who consequently killed his rival by hurling a rock at him. These are framed by Giovanni Battista Marchetti's ornamental motifs.

The large marble group of *Pluto and Proserpina* by Gian Lorenzo Bernini, shows Pluto, powerful god of the underworld, abducting Proserpina, daughter of Gea, earth. By interceding with Jupiter, her mother obtains permission for her daughter to return to earth for half the year and then spend the other half in Hades. Thus every spring the earth welcomes her with a carpet of flowers. The group was executed between 1621 and 1622. Cardinal Scipione gave it to Cardinal Ludovisi in 1622, and it remained in his villa until 1908, when it was purchased by the Italian state and returned to the Borghese Collection. In this group Bernini develops the twisting pose reminiscent of Mannerism, combined with an impression of vital energy (in pushing against Pluto's face Proserpina's hand creases his skin and his fingers sink into the flesh of his victim). Seen from the left, the group shows Pluto taking a fast and powerful stride and grasping Proserpina, from the front he appears triumphantly bearing his trophy in his arms; from the right one sees Proserpina's tears as she prays to heaven, the wind blowing her hair, as the guardian of Hades, the three-headed dog, barks. Various moments of the story are thus summed up in a single sculpture.

This group has often been said to strongly resemble ancient sculpture such as the *Niobe* (then in the Villa Medici), as regards Proserpina's face, while Pluto's stance is reminiscent of the *Pedagogue* (now in the Uffizi) and also the *Hercules Killing Hydra*, which was found in 1620 and restored by Algardi (now in the Capitoline Museums). Bernini, like Rubens, focussed on the tactile quality of his surfaces.

Already in antiquity, group sculptures were the most demanding task a sculptor could undertake. The *Farnese Bull* formerly in the courtyard of Palazzo Farnese in Rome (now in the Museo Archeologico, Naples) is a famous example of this. It represents the story of how Antiope, Amphion and Zethus punish

G. L. Bernini, *Pluto and Proserpina*, 1621-1622

G. L. Bernini, *Pluto and Proserpina*, detail, 1621-1622

Dirce for having mistreated their mother out of jealousy and tie her to a bull's horns. Scipione Borghese commissioned Antonio Susini (1613) to make a small bronze replica of this group by Apollonius and Taurscus from Tralles.

But the large marble groups by the Cardinal's sculptor, Bernini, were to excel any antique equivalent.

In the 18th century the porphyry and alabaster busts of the Roman emperors and the four vases in transparent marble decorated with amusing scenes of putti at play in all seasons, including ice-skating in winter, were executed by M. Laboureur and L. Cardelli in 1785. The theme of the four seasons reappears in the two hexagonal porphyry tables by Luigi Valadier with four refined gilded bronze masks on the base.

A. Susini, *The Farnese Bull* or *The Torture of Dirce*, 1613

Room V
Room of the Hermaphrodite

THE NYMPH ENCOUNTERS
HERMAPHRODITUS

CUPID AIMS HIS ARROW AT THE
NYMPH SALMACIS WHO
APPROACHES HERMAPHRODITUS

MERCURY AND
VENUS, PARENTS OF
HERMAPHRODITUS

HERMAPHRODITUS ASKING
HIS PARENTS TO CHANGE
THOSE WHO BATHE IN THE
RIVER SALMACIS INTO
HERMAPHRODITES

COMPANION
NYMPHS

SATYRS, HIDDEN
OBSERVERS

SLEEPING
HERMAPHRODITUS
WITH FAUN AND
SATYR

THE NYMPH SPYING ON
HERMAPHRODITUS

Pictures transferred to the ceiling: Nicola Bonvicini, 1781-1782
Decoration of the ceiling: Giovanni Battista Marchetti
Stucco putti: Vincenzo Pacetti

Sculptures: Hermaphrodite, 1st cent. AD, no. CLXXII / Porphyry Bath, 2nd-3rd cent. AD, reworked in 1778 by Paolo Santi from a drawing by A. Asprucci, no. CLXIV / Rare head of a Kore, 480-70 BC, no. CLXXXI / Head of Aphrodite (the so-called Sappho from Fidia), c.100 AD, no. CLXXXIV / Portrait of Agrippa the Elder, 37-41 AD, no. CLXXIX / 2 Roman satyrs playing the flute and pan-pipe, copy of an early Hellenistic original, no. CCXXVIII-CCXXVI /2 Statues of women, one of Ceres, 1st cent. AD and the other 2nd cent. AD, nos. CLXIX-CCXXXXII /Alabaster amphora by A. G. Granjacquet, 1783, no. CLXXIII.
Paintings: F. van Valckenborch, Landscape with St. Jerome, c.1596, no. 20 / P. Brill and assistant, Landscape with the Temple of the Sibyl, c.1595-1600, no. 12 / P. Brill and assistant, Fantastic Landscape, c.1595, no. 13 / P. Brill and assistant, Fantastic Landscape, c.1595, no. 19 / P. Brill and assistant, Landscape with Shepherds, c.1602, no. 21.

Hermaphrodite, 1st cent. AD, copy of an original by Polycles, 150 BC

At the time of Cardinal Borghese there existed an antique *Hermaphrodite* to which Bernini added a mattress and set it in a piece of wooden furniture with a door so as to hide its male and female parts from view. In 1807 it was sold to the Louvre and replaced by a second *Hermaphrodite*, found in 1781 and restored by V. Pacetti. This Parian marble work in the Borghese Gallery, dating from the 1st century AD, is a copy of an original by Polycles, who was active in Athens during the 2nd century BC. The scenes on the ceiling depicting the myth of the Hermaphrodite were painted by Nicola Bonvicini in 1781-1782. The large antique porphyry bath from Castel S. Angelo, reworked from a drawing by A. Asprucci in 1779, stands beside a Roman mosaic with fishing scenes, found at Castellarcione on the Via Tiburtina. The head of a *Kore*, deserves a special mention; it has bronze curls fitted into small holes drilled into the head and was executed in Magna Graecia at the beginning of the 5th century BC.

THE COUNCIL OF THE GODS ABOUT THE TROJAN WAR

IN FAVOUR:		AGAINST:
MINERVA	JUPITER	DIANA
THETIS		APOLLO
HEBE		IRIS
NEPTUNE		MARS
JUNO		VENUS
MERCURY		CUPID

Central painting: Laurent Pecheux, 1777-1783
Illusionist decorations: Giovanni Battista Marchetti
Stucco reliefs of Corybants: Vincenzo Pacetti

Sculptures: G. L. Bernini, Aeneas and Anchises, 1619-20, no. CLXXXII, and Truth, 1645-52, no. CCLXXVIII / Fr. Duquesnoy, Bacchanalia of Putti and Black Hunters, 1650-52, nos. CCLXXVI-CCLXXIV-CCLXXV / Sleeping Putti, 1609, artist unknown, no. CLXXXIV / Group of Aesclepius and Telesphorus, 2nd cent. AD, no. CIC / Nymph with a bowl, 2nd cent. AD, no. CIXC / Leda and the Swan, 130 AD, no. CVIIC, copy of an original by Timotheus, no. CVIIC / Colossal head of a divinity, 1st cent. AD / Eros in Chains and Boy with a Bird, 2nd cent. AD, copies of Hellenistic originals, nos. CXIII-CXV / Antique cameo with 17th-cent. additions with the head of Alexander the Great / Portrait bust of Paul V, artist unknown.
Paintings: G. M. Morandi, Death of the Virgin, preliminary sketch for the church of S. Maria della Pace / J. Zucchi, Cupid and Psyche, dated 1589, no. 10 / L. Fontana, Minerva Dressing, dated 1613, no. 7 / Alessandro Varotari, copy of, Cupid and Psyche, 19th cent., no. 52.

G. L. Bernini, *Aeneas and Anchises*, 1618-1620

Inspired by the antique sculpture of the famous *Borghese Gladiator*, formerly in this room and sold to Napoleon in 1807, the ceiling has been decorated with fighting scenes, particularly in the painting by Laurent Pecheux (1777-1783) in the Neoclassical style of the painter Mengs. It represents the *Council of the Gods* with the supporters and adversaries of Troy respectively on the right and the left of Jupiter. The dancing warriors, the so-called Corybants, in the reliefs by V, Pacetti derive from a similar antique example housed in the Museo Pio Clementino in the Vatican.

This room contains three celebrated works by Gian Lorenzo Bernini. In the centre stands the monument to the *Pietas romana*, the group sculpture *Aeneas and Anchises*, representing Aeneas fleeing from the burning city of Troy bearing

G. L. Bernini, *Aeneas and Anchises*, detail, 1618-1620

his elderly father Anchises on his shoulders, and his son Ascanius carrying the sacred fire of the hearth, while Anchises holds the *penates* or family household gods. The twenty-one-year-old Lorenzo Bernini, still influenced by his father Pietro's late sixteenth-century tower-shaped compositions, executed this group between 1618 and 1620, but many experts believe that this is mainly his father's work.

Bernini designed a work that was to be a monument to his sculptural art, *Truth Unveiled by Time*. The figure of Time that was intended for the upper part of the composition was never executed. This work was undertaken when Bernini was going through a difficult period at the papal court, because he was wrongly accused by his adversaries of causing structural problems at St Peter's. Bernini began preliminary work on *Truth* around 1645, at a critical time, after the death of Pope Urban VIII. By 1652, the figure was almost complete, but in 1665 Bernini again expressed his intention to add the figure of Time to the group. In his will Bernini bequeathed *Truth*, as an eternal warning, to his eldest son. The work remained in the Bernini home until 1924, when it was transferred to the Borghese Gallery and placed in Room VIII on a plinth slanting backwards (a stucco wedge had been added to the 19th-century base).

G. L. Bernini, *Truth*, 1645-1652

L. Fontana, *Minerva Dressing*, 1613

Recent restoration work has restored the base to its horizontal position, which gives *Truth* its original more erect pose. The powerful figure of *Truth*, which is reminiscent of Michaelangelo's deliberate contrast between smooth and unfinished parts and of the elegant physical tension of Rubens' female figures, can be considered the quintessence of Baroque sculpture, It is certainly Gian Lorenzo Bernini's most personal statue.

G. L. Bernini, *The Sun*, detail of *Truth*, 1645-1652

Room VII
Egyptian Room

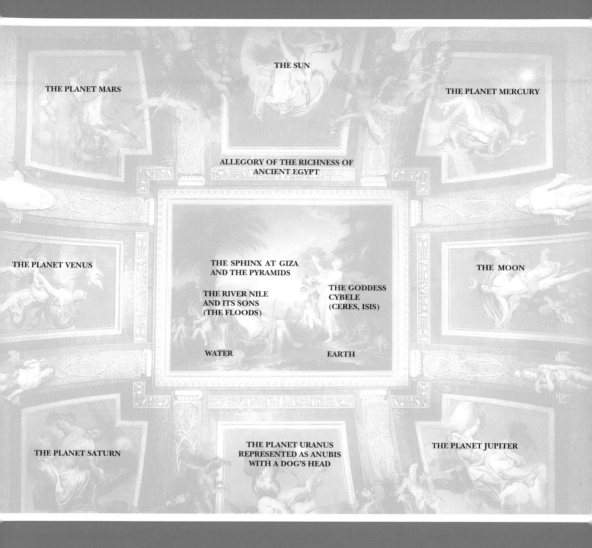

THE SUN

THE PLANET MARS

THE PLANET MERCURY

ALLEGORY OF THE RICHNESS OF
ANCIENT EGYPT

THE PLANET VENUS

THE SPHINX AT GIZA
AND THE PYRAMIDS

THE GODDESS
CYBELE
(CERES, ISIS)

THE RIVER NILE
AND ITS SONS
(THE FLOODS)

THE MOON

WATER

EARTH

THE PLANET SATURN

THE PLANET URANUS
REPRESENTED AS ANUBIS
WITH A DOG'S HEAD

THE PLANET JUPITER

Central painting and eight surrounding paintings: Tommaso Maria Conca, 1779-1780
Festoons: Giovanni de Pedibus
Illusionist decorations: Giovanni Battista Marchetti

Sculptures: in the centre, Satyr on a Dolphin, 1st cent. AD, copy of an original from Taranto, no. CC, head added and reworked in the 16th cent. / Peploflora, 1st cent. BC, copy of a 460 BC original, no. CCXVI / Bronze Isis with a lyre, 1st cent. AD, no. CCII / Paris, 1st cent. AD, copy of an original by Euphranorus, no. CCIII / Black marble Isis, c.150-60 AD, no. CCIX / Landolina-style Venus, 2nd cent. AD, no. CCXV / Statuette of Attis, 2nd cent. AD, no. LIX /Rosso antico goblet by L. Cardelli, c.1781, no. CCXXI / 4 Amphorae and 2 Vases in oriental alabaster, end of 18th cent. Frieze Paintings, circa 1780: T. Conca, Cleopatra's Banquet / The Dying Mark Antony / Cleopatra before Augustus / Death of Cleopatra / Sacrifice to Isis / Crocodile Hunt / Scenes of Apis worship / Egyptian landscapes.

The Egyptian Room, designed by A. Asprucci

Antonio Asprucci designed a room inspired by recurrent motifs in ancient Egyptian art to house the Borghese collection of Egyptian statues. Giovanni Battista Marchetti designed the painted ceiling and Tommaso Conca depicted the abundance of the land of the Nile, and the scenes of Antony and Cleopatra in Egypt linked to Roman history (1779-1782), beneath the cornice. A few years earlier, the taste for Egyptian art, launched by Piranesi's works, had also inspired the decoration of the Gabinetto dei Papiri in the Vatican Palace, where Egyptian statues were displayed. However, the perfection of this room in the Borghese Gallery was unrivalled and became a model for subsequent Egyptian rooms in Roman palazzi. After many statues were sent to Paris in 1807, the central place in the room was occupied by a celebrated ancient statue that Raphael had already studied in Rome over two centuries earlier: the *Satyr on a Dolphin*, dating from the 1st century AD, a copy of a Lysippus-style work executed in Taranto. The ancient head, which does not belong to the statue, was reworked in the early 16th century. The severe statue of a *Peploflora* (woman wearing a *peplos*) dates from the 5th century BC and is possibly

Peplofora, early 5th cent. BC

Isis, black marble 150 AD

a Greek original. The great *Isis* is represented as she hastens to seek the body of her husband Osiris and was sculpted in the mid-2nd century AD. Ancient Roman mosaics decorate the 'Egyptian' floor. The scene near the windows shows a purification rite in the month of March, when the priests, or *salii*, beat a boar's skin with rods before the statue of Mars, god of war.

Satyr on a Dolphin, 1st cent. AD, with head added later and reworked in the 16th cent.

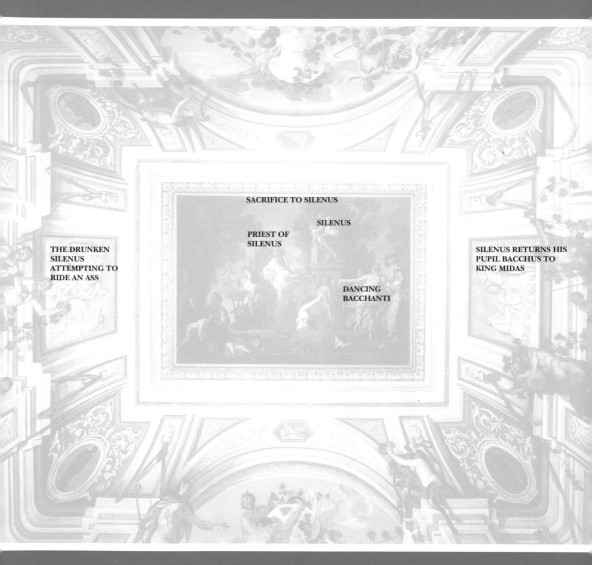

THE DRUNKEN
SILENUS
ATTEMPTING TO
RIDE AN ASS

SACRIFICE TO SILENUS

SILENUS

PRIEST OF
SILENUS

DANCING
BACCHANTI

SILENUS RETURNS HIS
PUPIL BACCHUS TO
KING MIDAS

Central painting and two chiaroscuro pictures, satyrs and putti on the cornice: Tommaso Maria Conca, 1775-1778
Illusionist decorations: Giovanni Battista Marchetti

Sculptures: Dancing Satyr, 2nd cent. AD, copy of an original by Lysippus, restored by Thorwaldsen, no CCXXV /Reliefs on the walls by T. Righi, 1778: Apollo and King Midas and Sacrifice / Seated statues: Mercury and a Philosopher, 1st cent. AD, no. CCXXXVII / Bust of Minerva, 17th cent., no. CCXXXI / Bust of Hygeia, 1st cent. AD, copy of a 400 BC original, no. LXXIII / Busts of Aesop (Pseudo Seneca), Tiberius, Germanicus, Domitia, Lucilla, Faustina the Elder, nos. CCXXX-CLXXV-CCXXXXIII-CCXXXXIV / Satyr in Repose, copy of an original by Praxiteles, 1st cent. AD, no. CCXXXII.
Paintings: Caravaggio: Il bacchino malato, 1592-95, no. 534; Boy with a Basket of Fruit, c. 1593-5, no. 136; Madonna of the Palafrenieri, 1605, no. 110; St. Jerome, 1605-6, no. 56; St. John the Baptist, 1609-10, no. 267; David with the Head of Goliath, 1609-10, no. 455 / Cavalier d'Arpino: The Capture of Christ, 1598, no. 356; The Rape of Europa, 1602-3, no. 378 / L. Cigoli, Joseph and Potiphar's Wife, 1610, no. 14 / G. Baglione, Judith and the Head of Holofernes, 1608, no. 15 / Master of the Judgement of Solomon, The Judgement of Solomon, c.1615-20, no. 33 / Dirk van Baburen, The Capture of Christ, 1616-17, no. 28.

Dancing Satyr, 2nd cent. AD, copy of a 4th-cent. BC original attrib. to Lysippus, restored by B. Thorwaldsen

This room is named after a famous antique group sculpture of *Silenus and Bacchus* (now in the Louvre) which was replaced by the *Dancing Satyr*, a Roman work in a twisting pose, in the 19th century. The Neoclassical sculptor, Berthel Thorvaldsen, restored the *Satyr*, but instead of the flute in the original attributed to Lysippus his figure is holding crotals, musical instruments similar to cymbals. The ceiling painting of the *Sacrifice to Silenus*, also depicts a bucolic subject and is brilliantly executed by Tommaso Conca, who was also responsible for the playful satyrs and putti framed by illusionist architectural motifs by Giovanni Battista Marchetti.

Room VIII contains six of the twelve paintings by Caravaggio, originally in the Cardinal's collection, including the *Supper at Emmaus* (now in the National Gallery, London). This large number of works in the Borghese collection indicates Cardinal Scipione's particular appreciation of this painter. On 16 April 1606, the large, new canvas of the *Madonna of the Palafrenieri* was removed from one of the most important altars in St. Peter's after only a month, because of its lack of 'decorum' and deviance from figurative tradition. It was then exhibited in Cardinal Borghese's collection in the hall of honour in the palazzo in the Borgo and later transferred to the entrance hall in the Villa Borghese. The novelty of this painting lies in the existential and human drama of the three figures facing danger. St. Anne, in antique style, detachedly contemplates the scene, as Mary teaches the young Jesus how to crush the serpent, symbol of sin and heresy. Darkness envelops the figures set in an undefined place, but an unnaturally bright light bursts forth from above bathing the child's skin in a warm glow. A month later Caravaggio was accused of murder and fled to distant lands (Naples, Sicily, Malta) to escape the price that had been placed on his head. His self-portrait as Goliath's severed head, held by David his executioner, was sent to the papal court in 1610 as a kind of painted petition for pardon. In fact pardon was granted, but did not reach Caravaggio before he died near Porto Ercole. In his *David with the Head of Goliath* Caravaggio pays tribute to the rapid brushstrokes Titian adopts in his later works and surrounds the youth's face with a kind of luminous halo that shines out from the dark, earthy tints surrounding the figure (see Titian's *St. Dominic*, Room XX).

The idea of existence being suspended between life and death is accentuated in the extraordinary painting of *St. Jerome* writing. On one side is a skull and a white, scythe-shaped cloth, on the other, the bald-headed saint sits wrapped in a bright red cloak. The strong horizontal line of the saint's arm holding the pen underlines the suspended effect and is like a sign of penitence.

There are two other major paintings dating from Caravaggio's early period in Rome, the *Boy with a Basket of Fruit* and the so-called *Bacchino malato* (young Bacchus ill). They date from the time when he left the studio of his influential contemporary the Cavalier d'Arpino and set up his own studio to paint not only still lifes of fruit and flowers, but above all human figures. But he was always equally committed to a realistic rendering of the most diverse subjects. Around 1592 the use of strong shadows had not yet entered

Caravaggio, *Madonna of the Palafrenieri*, 1605

Caravaggio, *St. Jerome*, 1605-1606

Caravaggio's paintings and a delicate chiaroscuro background, deriving from the Lombard school, acts as a counterpoint to the figures. The youth offers his guest a basket of fruit, the so-called *xenia* (gifts), according to the custom of the ancients, and the painter asserts his masterly skill, equal to that of ancient painters (like Zeuxis), who were capable of painting fruit that looked incredibly real. But his life-like approach to painting fruit and plants is new since their leaves are marked by their history. Caravaggio opened up a new chapter in that particular genre known as still life. His satirical self-portrait as *Il bacchino malato* is a tribute to artists' divine inspiration. That 'lunatic frenzy', the painter's creative urge, which manifests itself at night with the help of wine (*in vino veritas*) is seen in the pale 'lunar' flesh tones. Caravaggio's use of light and the immediacy of his figures must have influencd even his most classical contemporaries, as we can see from Guido Reni's *Moses* (Room XIV). Three paintings depicting violent scenes are placed together in this room, Baglione's *Judith with the Head of Holofernes*, Cigoli's *Joseph and Potiphar's Wife* and Caravaggio's *David with the Head of Goliath* and this reflects the arrangement in Cardinal Scipione's picture gallery in the palazzo in the Borgo, described by the poet Francucci in 1613. Caravaggio's influence soon spread on an international scale and can be seen in works like those by the master of the *Judgement of Solomon* and Dirk van Baburen's *Capture of Christ*. The Cavalier d'Arpino, Car-

Caravaggio, *Self-Portrait as Il bacchino malato*, c. 1593

Caravaggio, *Boy with a Basket of Fruit*, c. 1594

Caravaggio, *David with the Head of Goliath*, 1609-1610

Caravaggio, *St. John the Baptist*, c. 1609-1610

Cavalier d'Arpino, *The Capture of Christ*, 1596-1597

G. Baglione, *Judith with the Head of Holofernes*, 1608

L. Cigoli, *Joseph and Potiphar's Wife*, 1610

avaggio's contemporary in Rome, depicted the same subject in a skilful night-time painting on copper, which Bellori judged to be "the most beautiful work by the Cavaliere". It was this picture that inspired Caravaggio's cen-

trifugal composition in his *Martyrdom of St. Matthew* (in the church of San Luigi dei Francesi) and his depiction of the soldier pulling the garment off the last of the fleeing disciples in *The Capture of Christ* (National Gallery, Dublin).

Central scene: Vincenzo Berrettini, Ceres in a Chariot Drawn by Serpents, c.1788
Decorations: Giovanni Battista Marchetti

Paintings: Marcello Provenzale: Portrait of Paul V, 1621, no. 495; Orpheus, 1618, no. 492; Madonna and Child, c.1620, no. 498 / Johann Wilhelm Baur, View of Villa Borghese, dated 1636, no. 519 / Govaert van Schayck, attrib. to, View of Villa Borghese, c.1636-40, no. 573 / Jan Bruegel the Elder, follower of, Orpheus, end of 16th cent. beginning of 17th cent., no. 278 / Paul Brill, View of a Port, 1610, no. 354; Seascape, 1595, no. 513 / Hendrik Cornelisz Vroom, attrib. to, Naval Battle in 1588 against the Invincible Armada, 1588-90, no. 345 / Jan Bruegel the Elder, attrib. to, Flowers, 1595, no. 362 / Ludovico Leone, called Il Padovano, Portrait of Pope Paul V Borghese, beginning of 17th cent., no. 73 / Tuscan Masters: The Sacrifice of Isaac, beginning of the 17th cent., no. 490; The Promised Land, beginning of the 17th cent. no. 494; The Penitent Mary Magdalen, 17th cent., no. 491; The Madonna as a Washerwoman, 17th cent. no. 493; Augustine's Vision, 17th cent., no. 477 / Jan Bruegel the Elder, Flowers, c.1593, no. 516.

Pictures that are of particular historical interest, since they show the original Villa Borghese, introduce the visitor to the rooms on the picture gallery floor. What the villa looked like in Cardinal Borghese's time can be seen in J. W. Baur's extraordinarily fine and realistic view of the façade of the villa and its lively forecourt, executed in tempera on parchment in 1636. The other view which renders the 'atmosphere' of the villa is attributed to Govaert van Schayck and derives from a rather vague memory embellished with many imaginary elements. A miniature mosaic by Marcello Provenzale praises Cardinal Scipione (whose marble bust by Bernini can be seen in Room XIV) allegorically as the 'new Orpheus', accompanied by the Borghese eagle and dragon, by alluding to his well-known capacity as mediator at the Roman court. Provenzale executed a life-like mosaic portrait of *Pope Paul V Borghese* of such outstanding quality that it technically surpasses those of antiquity; he 'painted' even his hair in mosaic tesserae. He also skilfully captured the glittering light on the halos in his mosaic of the *Madonna and Child*. In the *View of a Port* by Paul Brill the ships are flying the Borghese flag, while the *Fall of Lucifer* by Palma il Giovane refers to Venice and its conflicts with Rome at the time of Pope Paul V. Works executed in semi-precious stones and small decorative branches indicate the variety of objects in the collection.

M. Provenzale, *Scipione Borghese as Orpheus*, 1608

Room IX
Room of Dido, formerly Room of the Three Graces

MERCURY EXHORTS AENEAS TO
LEAVE CARTHAGE

AENEAS FLEES FROM
THE FLAMES OF TROY

DIDO'S SUICIDE

DIDO'S BANQUET WITH
AENEAS AND ACATE

AENEAS AND HIS COMPANION
ACATE APPEAR BEFORE DIDO

Pictures transferred to the ceiling: Anton von Maron, 1783-1785
Illusionist decorations: Giovanni Battista Marchetti
Fireplace: Vincenzo Pacetti, 1783

Paintings: Raphael: Portrait of a Lady with a Unicorn, c.1506, no. 371; Portrait of a Man, 1502-4, no. 307; The Deposition, 1507, no. 369/ The Baker's Daughter, copy after Raphael, Raffaellino del Colle attrib. to, mid-16th cent., no. 355 /Raphael, copy of, Portrait of Pope Julius II, 16th cent., no. 413 / Fra Bartolomeo and Mariotto Bertinelli, The Holy Family with the Infant St. John the Baptist, dated 1511, no. 310 / Perugino, attrib. to, St. Sebastian, after 1490, no. 386 / Ridolfo del Ghirlandaio, Portrait of a Youth, beginning of 16th cent., no. 399 / Lambert van Noort, attrib. to, Psyche Taken to Olympus, c.1540, no. 184 / H. Schäuffelein, attrib. to, Portrait of a Man, dated 1505, no. 287 / Perin del Vaga, The Holy Family with the Infant St. John the Baptist and St. Anne, mid-16th cent., no. 412 / Fra Bartolomeo, attrib. to, Christ Blessing, c. 1505, no. 421 / Lorenzo di Credi, Madonna and Child with the Infant St. John the Baptist, 1488-95, no. 433 / Perin del Vaga, The Holy Family, c.1540, no. 464 / Pier Francesco Foschi, Tobias and the Angel, c.1545, no. 173 / Raffaellino del Colle, Madonna and Child with the Infant St. John the Baptist, c. 1530, no. 320 / Piero di Cosimo, The Adoration of the Christ Child, after 1510, no. 343 / Botticelli and assistants, Madonna and Child, the Infant St. John the Baptist and Angels, c.1488, no. 348 / Jacopo del Tedesco, attrib. to, The Adoration of the Christ Child, no. 352 / Giulio Romano, Virgin and Child with the Infant St. John the Baptist, c.1523, no. 374 / Pinturicchio, attrib. to, The Crucifixion with St. Christopher and St. Jerome, before 1473, no. 377 / Perugino, Madonna and Child, early 16th cent., no. 401 / Fra Bartolomeo, The Adoration of the Christ Child, c.1495, no. 439.
In the centre, a yellow alabaster goblet on verde antique marble columns, c.1781.

Raphael, *The Deposition*, 1507

This room contains works by 16th-century Florentine and Umbrian masters, culminating in Raphael, whose followers in Rome were Perin del Vaga, Giulio Romano, Machuca and Raffaellino dal Colle. One of Fra Bartolomeo's finest works is the tondo depicting *The Adoration of the Christ Child*, whose particularly poetic atmosphere makes it possible to date it from circa 1499. The meaningful composition combines the movement of the figures in an extraordinary chiaroscuro that highlights and links the drapery, faces and background landscape. This work, as R. Longhi has pointed out, draws its inspiration from Verrocchio and Leonardo. Another remarkable tondo dating from the beginning of the 16th century is *The Adoration of the Christ Child* by Piero di Cosimo, in which the unusual wedge-shaped composition places the Christ Child and cross in the foreground, while worshipping angels and St. Joseph are seen in the background with a grazing ass and bull. The valuable small panel depicting *The Crucifixion with*

Pinturicchio, *The Crucifixion with St. Jerome and St. Christopher*,

St. Jerome and St Christopher (c.1471) was painted by the young Pinturicchio and reflects his experience as a miniaturist. This master, like Perugino (whose *Madonna and Child* and attributed *St. Sebastian* are exhibited here), was to have a great influence on Raphael and so were northern masters. In fact in the 19th century Raphael's *Portrait of a Man* which can be dated to the period of his youth (c.1502), was thought to be by Holbein and then by Perugino, until Giovanni Morelli met with general consensus by attributing it to Raphael. This portrait, probably of a duke given the shape of the hat, is idealized in the perfect modelling of the volumes, flowing hair and vivid expression. The approach is very different from the realistic style of the northern painters, who sought to include all the true-to-life details including defects, as in the dishevelled *Portrait of a Man*, 1505, attributed to H. Schauffelein, but formerly thought to be by Dürer. The portrait of Raphael's mysterious *Lady with a Unicorn*, circa 1506, had been heavily painted

Perugino, *Madonna and Child*, beginning of the 16th

Raphael, *Lady with a Unicorn*, c.1506

Raphael, *Portrait of a Man*, c.1502

H. Schäuffelin, attrib. to, *Portrait of a Man*, 1505

Fra Bartolomeo, *The Adoration of the Christ Child*, c.1499

over to represent a St. Catherine at the time of R. Longhi (1928), who identified the artist. After careful cleaning, the perfect geometry and detachment of this courtly figure were revealed, though her identity is not known. Leonardo, Piero della Francesca and Perugino influences have been noted in the style of the painting.

Raphael's *Deposition* was painted for Atalanta Baglioni in memory of her son Grifonetto, who was killed in the fighting for the dominance of Perugia, and housed in the church of S. Francesco in Perugia in 1507. It remained there for 101 years, until it was removed at night with the complicity of the priest and sent to Pope Paul V, who gave it to his nephew for his collection and it thus became the property of the Borghese family. After the Treaty of Tolentino the painting was sent to Paris in 1797. When it came back to Rome in 1816, only the central scene was returned to the Borghese collection, while the three theological virtues, Faith, Hope and Charity, remained in the Vatican Museums (the ornamentation surmounting it by Tiberio Alfani is in the Galleria Nazionale of Umbria). This large altarpiece presents the scene like a Roman relief and is inspired by the reliefs on ancient Roman sarophagi depicting the transportation of Meleager. It is interesting to note that in his preliminary sketch the artist had drawn Christ lying on the ground, as in the painting by Perugino,

but when he executed the painting he decided on the antique form of transportation, as seen in a relief he probably studied on the Montalvo sarcophagus in Florence (now in the Torno Collection, Milan). But the influence of Michelangelo can also be seen in the composition of Christ (cf. the *Pietà*, St. Peter's) and the figure seen in profile supporting the Madonna repeats a similar pose in the *Doni Tondo* (in the Uffizi, completed a year before *The Deposition*.). The copies of a painting by Raphael depicting his patron Pope Julius II, by an unknown artist (original lost) and the beautiful *Fornarina*, a fine painting by his pupil Raffaellino dal Colle (original reworked by Giulio Romano, now in Palazzo Barberini), recall influential figures in Raphael's life.

Piero di Cosimo, *The Adoration of the Christ Child,* 1505

Room X
Room of Hercules or Room of Sleep

ALLEGORY OF
FORTITUDE

HERCULES PUNISHES LICA
FOR BRINGING HIM THE
POISONED ROBE

ALLEGORY OF JUSTICE

DEATH OF HERCULES

THE APOTHEOSIS OF HERCULES:
TRANSFORMED INTO AN EAGLE
MERCURY TAKES HIM TO OLYMPUS
WHERE HE IS RECEIVED BY JUPITER
AND JUNO

THE CENTAUR NESSUS
CARRIES OFF DEIANIRA

ALLEGORY OF
TEMPERANCE

HERCULES RECEIVES FROM THE NAIADS
THE HORN OF HIS DEFEATED
ADVERSARY, ACHELOUS

ALLEGORY OF
PRUDENCE

Pictures transferred to the ceiling: Christoph Unterberger, 1784-1786
Illusionist decorations: Giovanni Battista Marchetti
Fireplace, white marble and porphyry: Vincenzo Pacetti

Sculptures: N. Cordier, The Gypsy, 1607-12 no. CCLXIII
Paintings: Andrea del Sarto, Madonna and Child with the Infant St. John the Baptist, 1517-18, no. 334 / Luca Cambiaso, Venus and Cupid, 1560-65, no. 123; Cupid in Repose, 1560-65, no. 191; Venus and Adonis, 1565-68, no. 317 / Correggio, Danäe, 1530-31, no. 125 / Nicolò dell'Abate, Portrait of a Woman, mid-16th cent., no. 77; Landscape with Ladies and Knights, 1550-52, no. 6 / Parmigianino, follower of, Portrait of a Youth, 1630s, no. 86 / Girolamo da Carpi, Portrait of a Man Holding Gloves, c. mid-16th cent., no. 97 / Michele di Ridolfo del Ghirlandaio, Lucretia, c.1560-70, no. 322; Leda and the Swan, c.1560-70, no. 323 / Pier Francesco Foschi, attrib. to, The Judgement of Solomon, early 16th cent., no. 329 / Bronzino, St. John the Baptist, c.1525, no. 444 / Girolamo da Carpi, attrib. to, Landscape with Magicians, c.1525, no. 8 / Parmigianino, Portrait of a Man, 1528-30, no. 85 / Pordenone, attrib. to, Judith, c.1516, no. 91 / Lelio Orsi, St. Cecily and St. Valerian, 1680s, no. 167 / Dosso Dossi, follower of, David with the Head of Goliath and a Page, 17th cent., no. 181 / Venus and Two Cupids, 1525, no. 324 / Lucas Cranach the Elder, Venus and Cupid with a Honeycomb, c.1531, no. 326.

L. Cranach, *Venus and Cupid with a Honeycomb*, c.1531

In the 17th century this room was called the Room of Sleep, because it housed a four-poster bed, a celestial globe and the black marble group by the sculptor Alessandro Algardi, the allegory of *Sleep*, representing a boy with butterfly wings holding poppies, accompanied by two large vases with handles in the form of serpents (see Room XIV). Standing in the centre of the room is the smiling *Gypsy* by Nicolas Cordier, executed between 1607 and 1612 for Cardinal Scipione, as can be seen from the eagles and dragons decorating the hem of her gown. This statue consists of an ancient grey marble torso to which Cordier added the elegant sections in white marble and gilded bronze (recent restoration has revealed the gold clasp by removing a thick black patina, which toned down its splendour to suit 19th-century taste). The early 16th-century paintings in this room are by Florentine masters and painters from the Parma, Bologna, Brescia and Genoa schools, and include a *Venus* by Cranach and a *Venus* by Brescianino, which were displayed together in Cardinal Scipione's collection.

Brescianino (a painter active in Siena and a follower of Andrea del Sarto in his rendering of atmospheres) painted the *Venus* around 1525, creating the illusion of a life-like figure looking into the mirror in the seashell as though about to step out of the niche, and flanked by cupids with tousled hair.

Around 1531, Cranach (a leading painter of the German Renaissance, who had trained in Flemish studios) on the other hand, painted a *Venus* draped in a transparent veil gazing directly at the spectator, whose refined flowing lines are far-removed from the style of ancient statues. The fine brushwork captures every wrinkle in the bark of the tree and every feather in the wings. Cranach decided to accompany his nude figure with a moralizing couplet by the Humanist Chelidonius which reminds us that *voluptas* is transitory and accompanied by pain, as the little Cupid realizes when he tastes the honey-

A. Brescianino, *Venus and Two Cupids*, c.1520-1525

Ferrarese master, attrib. to Girolamo da Carpi, *Landscape with Magicians*, c.1525

Nicolò dell'Abate, *Deer Hunt*, c.1550-1552

comb with its stinging bees. Correggio's masterpiece, *Danäe*, depicts one of the four stories in Ovid's *Metamorphoses* about the "loves of Jupiter", commissioned in around 1531 by Frederick II Gonzaga in Mantua as a present for Charles V (the other scenes are in the Kunst-historisches Museum, Vienna and the National Gallery, London). Jupiter, transformed into a golden shower, is received by Cupid and Danäe, while heavenly and earthly love test the metal of the point of love's arrow with a goldsmith's stone. Correggio, a sophisticated naturalist painter at the time of Mannerism, has always been celebrated for the subtle shades, and imperceptible changes of tone he created by using subtle glazing. The picture's soft sensuality fascinated many European courts, in fact, it had a number of different owners and travelled to Madrid (1532), Milan (1584),

N. Cordier, *The Gypsy*, c.1607-1612

Prague (1621), Stockholm (1652), Rome (1654), Paris (1721), Brussels (1792), England (1798), Paris (beginning of the nineteenth century) and Rome (1827). This work's Odyssey of journeys and restoration work explains the gaps in the pictorial surface and the loss of glazing, though its former splendour can still be appreciated.

Two paintings that were above the doors in Room II until the late 19th century, can now be seen by the public. They are the brilliant *Deer Hunt* by Nicolò dell'Abate, talented exponent of the Bolognese 'manner', and the *Landscape with Magicians* from the Ferrara school, attributed to Girolamo da Carpi, in which echoes of Bosch's surreal world are evident.

Andrea del Sarto painted the large *Madonna and Child with the Infant St. John the Baptist*, 1515-1517, for the Florentine businessman Giovanni Gaddi, a work

Andrea del Sarto, *Madonna and Child with the Infant St. John the Baptist*, 1515-1517

Correggio, *Danäe*, c.1531

that was not completed until a decade after his elegant altarpiece with the *Pietà* (Room IX), in this gallery. But here his formal language has completely changed; he adopts dramatically twisting poses, views from above and from below, a complex series of movements and a light that 'sculpts' the bodies rendering them in full relief. 'Florentine Mannerism' is the term used to describe this style of painting. Bronzino's *St. John the Baptist* reflects this new trend even more strongly, which is marked by disorientation and the traumatic political and cultural events that accompanied the passage from Republican forms of

A. Algardi, *Sleep*, c.1635

Parmigianino, *Portrait of a Man*, 1528-1530   A. Bronzino, *St. John the Baptist*, c.1525

government to the domination of the Medici court. St. John the Baptist is depicted in the desert, proud in gesture, colour and light, but the strained twisting pose of his body gives him an undeniable air of pathos.

Room XI

GANYMEDE ABDUCTED BY JUPITER   COUNCIL OF THE GODS WITH THE
PRESENTATION OF GANYMEDE   GANYMEDE JUPITER'S CUP-BEARER

Central scenes: Vincenzo Berrettini, 1790
Decorations: Felice Giani

Paintings: Scarsellino: The Massacre of the Innocents, end of 16th cent. beginning of 17th cent., no. 209; Salmacis and Hermaphroditus, c.1585, no. 214; Venus Bathing, before 1585, no. 219; Supper at the House of Simon the Pharisee, 1590-95, no. 169; Venus and Adonis, beginning of 17th cent., no. 212 / Garofalo: Virgin and Child, with St. Michael and other Saints, c.1530-32, no. 240; The Holy Family, early 16th cent., no. 409; Madonna and Child with St. Peter and St. Paul, c.1520, no. 213; The Adoration of the Shepherds, after c.1510, no. 224; The Scourging of Christ, c.1540, no. 237; The Conversion of St. Paul, dated 1545, no. 347 / Garofalo, follower of: Christ and the Samaritan at the Well, mid-16th cent., no. 235; "Noli me tangere", late 16th cent., no. 244 / Mazzolino: The Adoration of the Magi, c.1522, no. 218; The Incredulity of St. Thomas, 1520-21, no. 223; The Nativity, 1506-10, no. 247; Christ and the Adultress, 1527, no. 451 / Ortolano, The Deposition, c.1520, no. 390.

This room is devoted to Cardinal Scipione's large number of works from the Ferrara school of painting. The market for Ferrarese art had become particularly favourable, since Ferrara came under the direct sovereignty of the Church in 1597. Cardinal Enzo Bentivoglio's involvement also facilitated the transfer of works from Ferrara to Rome. The paintings of the Ferrarese Renaissance on exhibit here (by Mazzolino, Garofalo and Ortolano, whereas Dossi's works are to be found in Room XV and Room III) share a particularly sensitive observation of nature and the expressive features of the landscape, which play a role in the picture, as in the dramatic *Mourning the Dead Christ* by Ortolano (1520-1521), but also in the refined small panels by Mazzolino (see the painting in which doubting Thomas touches Christ's wounds, as a new vision opens before him expressed in the vibrant celestial landscape). The large canvas (formerly on a panel) of the turbulent *Conversion of St. Paul on the Road to Damascus* is by Garofalo. It was painted in 1545 and illustrates how the fragile Raphaelesque harmony in the works of the previous decade had been shattered by the influence of Giulio Romano in Mantua, for example in the *Madonna with St. Michael and other Saints* or in the poetic *Madonna between St. Peter and St. Paul* (c.1520) from the period of his early maturity.

L. Mazzolino, *The Incredulity of St. Thomas*, c.1522

Ortolano, *Mourning the Dead Christ*, 1520-1521

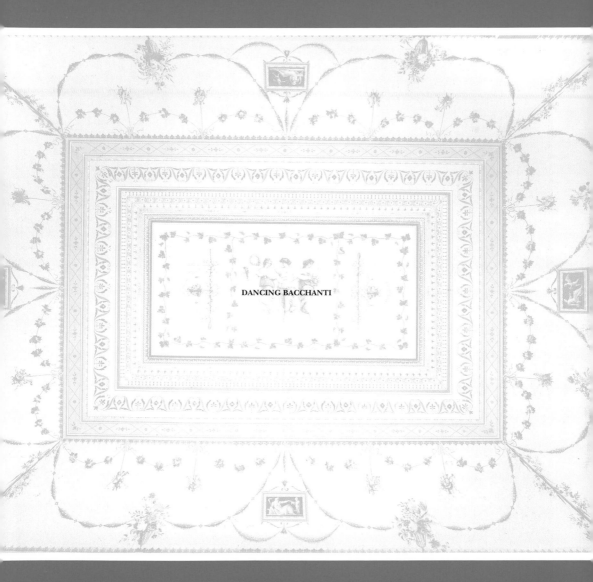

DANCING BACCHANTI

Wall paintings: Felice Giani, 1790

Paintings: G. A. Boltraffio, Portrait of a Woman, beginning of 16th cent., no. 151 / Sodoma: The Holy Family, 1525-30, no. 459; Pietà, c.1540, no. 462 / Baldassarre Peruzzi, Venus, early 16th cent., no. 92 / Lorenzo Lotto, Portrait of Mercurio Bua, c.1535, no. 185 / Simon de Châlons: Our Lady of Sorrows, dated 1543, no. 280; Ecce Homo, 1543, no. 286 / Leonardo, copy of, Leda and the Swan, early 16th cent., no. 434 / Marco d'Oggiono, Christ Blessing, c.1500, no. 435 / Domenico Beccafumi, drawing, Head of a Youth for the scene of the sacrifice of Zaleucus in the Sala del Concistoro in the Palazzo Pubblico, Siena, 1530-35, no. 453 / Giampietrino, Madonna Nursing the Christ Child, mid-16th cent., no. 456 / Andrea Solario, Christ Carrying the Cross, c.1524, no. 461 / Master of the Sforza Altarpiece, drawing, Head of a Woman, beginning of 16th cent. no. 514 / Bartolomeo Vivarini, attrib. to, Madonna and Child, late 15th cent., no. 578.

Sodoma, *Pietà*, c. 1540

This room contains early 15th-century works from Lombardy, Veneto and the Siena area, whose atmosphere and dynamic movement indicate the influence of Leonardo. In the inventories, the famous painting of *Leda and the Swan* was for three hundred years (until 1893) thought to be by Sodoma, or a copy by the latter (Longhi). Its attribution is still doubtful, but from recent research into wills it is now thought to be an unfinished painting that was in Leonardo's house at the time of his death (1519) and inherited by his pupil Salaì who re-worked it. X-rays have revealed another composition beneath this one depicting Leda's four children (Castor, Pollux, Helen and Clytemnestra) emerging from the swan's eggs. Leda with her arms around the swan (Jupiter) in an elegant curving pose, her hair partially escaping from her plaits, set against the spacious river landscape, was most certainly conceived by Leonardo, but executed by different artists.

The *Christ Blessing* by Marco d'Oggiono and the *Madonna* by Giampietrino were also thought to be by Leonardo. In the latter picture, the Madonna is intent on feeding the Christ Child, but He is pulling away in a spiral movement - a movement which Leonardo observed in natural phenom-

Copy after Leonardo, *Leda and the Swan*, early 16th cent.

ena in the dynamics of water, wind, plants and human figures. The *Christ Carrying the Cross* by Andrea Solario is a copy of a famous drawing by Leonardo in Venice (Galleria dell'Accademia) and the French artist Simon de Chalons was influenced by Leonardo through Solario's copies of his works in the diptych of the *Our Lady of Sorrows* and the *Ecce Homo*. One of the three paintings by the Sienese artist Sodoma, the *Pietà* was celebrated in the 17th century as the work of Leonardo, and current criticism still sees echoes of Leonardo in his chiaroscuro atmospheres and harmonious rhythms. A rare drawing of a *Head* by D. Beccafumi is a preliminary study for the figure in the fresco in the Palazzo Pubblico in Siena depicting the sacrifice of Zaleucus, whereas the other drawing, formerly thought to be by Leonardo, is attributed to the Master of the Pala Sforzesca and illustrates the elegance and fine modelling of the figures drawn with a silver point, a technique common in the Lombard school. Two large portraits that are more than simple representations come from the Brescia area and are influenced by the Veneto and Lombard schools. The melancholy *Portrait of a Man* by Lorenzo Lotto is

L. Lotto, *Portrait of a Man*, c.1535

probably the portrait of the widower, Mercurio Bua, because of the small skull surrounded by rose petals, reminiscent of a fatal confinement. The painter of the enigmatic *Portrait of a Woman* has not yet been identified (Longhi thought it resembled Lotto's style and could be dated to c.1530).

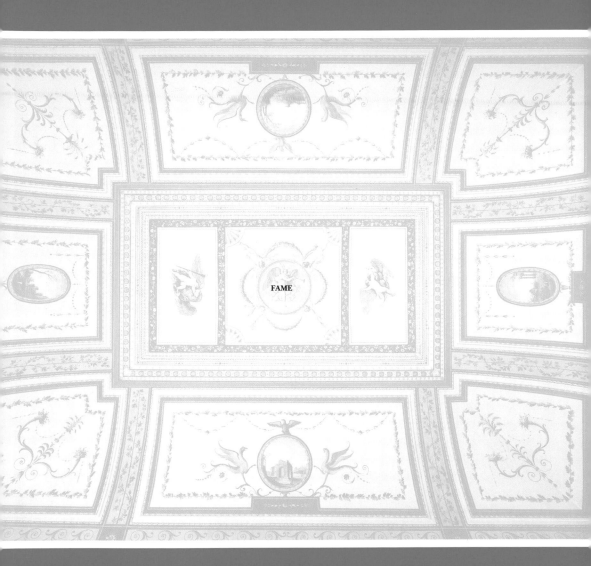

FAME

Decorations: Felice Giani, 1790

Paintings: Francesco Bonsignore, reworking of, Portrait of Petrarch, end of 15th cent., no. 426 / Domenico Puligo: The Holy Family, c.1526, no. 432; Virgin and Child with Two Angels, 1512-15, no. 468; Mary Magdalen, c.1526, no. 328 / Francesco Francia: St. Francis, c.1510, no. 57; Madonna and Child, c.1510, no. 61; St. Stephen, 1475, no. 65 / Francesco Francia, follower of, Madonna and Child, c.1520, no. 34 / Bernardino Fungai, Communion of St. Catherine of Siena, end of 15th cent., no. 228 / Kress Master of Landscapes, Madonna and Child with St. Joseph and the Infant St. John the Baptist, c.1515, no. 332 / Lorenzo Costa, The Scourging of Christ, before 1492, no. 395 / Antonio di Donnino del Mazziere, attrib. to, Stories of Joseph: Jacob Learns of Joseph's Presumed Death, c.1523, no. 463 / Bachiacca, Stories of Joseph the Jew: The Arrest of Joseph's Brothers, 1515-16, no. 425; Stories of Joseph the Jew: The Selling of Joseph, 1515-16, no. 427; Stories of Giuseppe the Jew: The Search for the Stolen Goblet, 1515-16, no. 440; Stories of Joseph the Jew: The Discovery of the Stolen Goblet, 1515-16, no. 442 / Franciabigio, Francesco di Cristofano, Madonna and Child with the Infant St. John the Baptist, dated 1518, no. 458 / Alonso Berruguete, Madonna and Child with the Infant St. John the Baptist and St. Elisabeth, 1508-14, no. 335 / Pedro Machuca, The Holy Family, c.1518, no. 174.

This room contains late 15th-century and early 16th-century works by Bolognese and Florentine masters. Grouped together here are artists who shared an interest in draughtsmanship and the rationally studied, harmonious proportions of the human figure and its measured pose, whose outlines distinguish it from its setting. The figures in the paintings by Francesco Francia, leading artist of the Bolognese school, have a delicate meditative expression as can be seen in the *Madonna and Child in the Rose Garden*. The *Scourging of Christ* with His direct intense gaze is by his teacher Lorenzo Costa. The *Five Stories of Joseph* were formerly in the famous Camera Borgherini, the panelled bridal room, decorated in Florence between 1515 and 1518 by the best painters of the day, including Andrea del Sarto, Pontormo, Granacci and others. Cardinal Scipione only managed to remove the four smaller side scenes by Francesco Ubertini, known as Il Bacchiacca, for his collection while the rest remained intact until the Napoleonic period (later the Borghese Gallery acquired the largest scene, documented in 1833, the other sections are now in the National Gallery, London, the Uffizi and Palazzo Pitti, Florence). Eccentric trends and experiments in composition that verged on a distortion of formal equilibrium soon began to take place in Florence and these culminated in the emergence of Mannerism. This style was evident in the *Madonna* attributed to the Kress Master

Kress master of landscapes, *Madonna and Child with St. Joseph and the Infant St. John the Baptist*, c1512

of Landscapes by F. Zeri and dating from circa 1512 or attributed to Rosso Fiorentino by R. Longhi, and now reconsidered by more recent criticism.

Fra Bartolomeo, a Dominican active in the monastery and school of S. Marco in Florence, executed the subtle painting of *Christ Blessing* (c.1516), inspired by the painting of the Flemish artist Memling as recent studies of the work have demonstrated, whereas *The Holy Family*, bearing the seal of the cross and two rings of Fra Bartolomeo's studio in Florence (see also the tondo in Room IX), has been attributed to Mariotto Albertinelli.

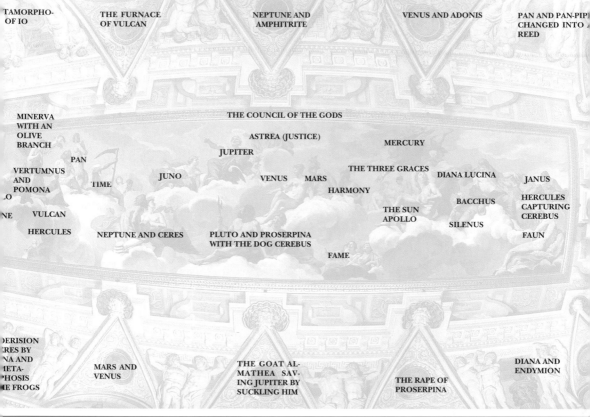

TAMORPHO-
OF IO

THE FURNACE
OF VULCAN

NEPTUNE AND
AMPHITRITE

VENUS AND ADONIS

PAN AND PAN-PIP
CHANGED INTO A
REED

MINERVA
WITH AN
OLIVE
BRANCH

THE COUNCIL OF THE GODS

ASTREA (JUSTICE)

MERCURY

PAN

JUPITER

VERTUMNUS
AND
POMONA

JUNO

THE THREE GRACES

DIANA LUCINA

JANUS

TIME

VENUS

MARS

HARMONY

HERCULES
CAPTURING
CEREBUS

VULCAN

THE SUN
APOLLO

BACCHUS

HERCULES

SILENUS

FAUN

NEPTUNE AND CERES

PLUTO AND PROSERPINA
WITH THE DOG CEREBUS

FAME

DERISION
RES BY
NA AND
META-
PHOSIS
E FROGS

MARS AND
VENUS

THE GOAT AL-
MATHEA SAV-
ING JUPITER BY
SUCKLING HIM

THE RAPE OF
PROSERPINA

DIANA AND
ENDYMION

Ceiling: Giovanni Lanfranco, The Council of the Gods, 1624
Five lunettes with rivers and wall scenes: Domenico Corvi, 1890s

Sculptures: G. L. Bernini: The Goat Almathea, 1615 or earlier no. CXVIII; Bust of Pope Paul V, c.1618 no. CCXLVIII; 2 Portraits of Cardinal Scipione Borghese, c.1632 nos. CCLXV-CCLXVI; Model for the Equestrian Statue of Louis XIV, 1669-70 no. CCLXIX / Antique group of an Amazon with a Barbarian and a Greek, 160-180 AD no. CCXLV / Eros Sleeping, 2nd cent. AD no. CVIIIC / Deer, 2nd cent. AD no. CXCII./ A. Algardi, Sleep, c.1635 no. CLX / Bust of a boy, 1st-2nd cent. AD. no. CCLX

Paintings: Francesco Albani, Tondos of the Four Seasons, 1616-17, nos. 35, 40, 44, 49 / Guido Reni, Moses with the Tables of the Law, beginning of 17th cent., no. 180 / Paul Brill: Landscape with the Baptism of Christ and St. John the Baptist Preaching, c.1597, no. 258; The Killing of St. Peter the Martyr, c.1597, no. 263 / G. L. Bernini: Self-Portrait as a Mature Man, c. 1630-35, no. 545; Self-Portrait as a Young Man, c.1623, no. 554; Portrait of a Boy, c.1638, no. 555 / Gio. Battista Viola. Landscape, dated 1613, no. 25 / Gerrit van Honthorst, Concert, 1620-27, no. 31 / Gio. Francesco Grimaldi: Landscape with a Scene in a Tent, c.1678, no. 38; Landscape with Fishermen, c.1678, no. 47; Landscape with a Waterfall, c.1678, no. 296; Landscape with St. John the Baptist Preaching, c.1678, no. 299 / Lionello Spada, Concert, c.1615, no. 41 / Guercino, The Prodigal Son, c.1627-28, no. 42 / Jacques Stella, Judith, c.1612, no. 261 / Orbetto: Christ in the Sepulchre, 1616-17, no. 307; The Dead Christ with Mary Magdalen and Angels, c.1617, no. 499; The Raising of Lazarus, 1615-17, no. 506 / Pomarancio, The Holy Family with Angels, 1602-5, no. 330 / Marcantonio Bassetti, The Deposition, 1613-16, no. 431 / Pasquale Ottino, The Raising of Lazarus, c.1614, no. 507 / After Guercino, Samson Offering a Honeycomb, c. 1626, no. 70 / Pier Francesco Mola, attrib. to, St. Peter Freed from Prison, c.1640-50, no. 192 / Paul Brill studio, Landscape with St. Francis, c.1595, no. 252 / Pomarancio, attrib. to, Cristoforo Roncalli, The Holy Family, c.1580, no. 365 / Cavalier d'Arpino, Battle of Tullius Ostilius against the Veientes, c.1600, no. 391 / Cristoforo Allori, St. Francis Praying, c.1610, no. 407.

G. L. Bernini, *Self-Portrait as a Mature Man*, c.1630-1635

This large room, decorated in 1624 with the fresco of the *Council of the Gods* by Giovanni Lanfranco, was originally an open loggia, but it was closed in the late 18th century, when Domenico Corvi restored the ceiling and added the paintings on the walls and arches.

This room is devoted to works from the second decade of the 17th century. The great fathers of Baroque painting Annibale Carracci (1602), Caravaggio and Elsheimer (1610) had just died, and Rubens had returned to Flanders. The followers of Caravaggio and Carracci vied with each other for predominance and their diverse styles can be seen here. Some sought a classical approach and a serene harmony of forms and colours, others were intent on humbly capturing simple everyday life set in a powerful contrast of light and shadow. But there was no hard and fast dividing line between them and even classical painters like Guido Reni in his *Moses* and Guercino in the *Prodigal Son*, are influenced by Caravaggio's heroic dramatic style. This new humble yet monumental language became an international phenomenon, as can be seen, for example, in the *Concert* by Honthorst or the imposing *St. Peter Freed from Prison*, better attributed to Le Valentin, as in the 1693 inventory, rather than to Mola as is believed today. The night scene depicting *Lot and his Daughters* by Giovan Francesco Guerrieri also shows Caravaggio's influence. On the walls by the windows are paintings on slate by a group of artists from Verona: Alessandro Turchi (known as L'Orbetto), Pasquale Ottini and Marcantonio Bassetti, who brought some of Caravaggio's innovations to northern Italy.

Francesco Albani, an exponent of the

G. L. Bernini, *Self-Portrait as a Young Man*, c.1623

G. L. Bernini, *Portrait of a Boy*, c.1638

G. L. Bernini, *Terracotta Model for the Equestrian Statue of King Louis XIV*, 1669-1670

G. L. Bernini, *The Goat Almathea*, before 1615

classical ideal, chose a format for his four tondos which, in his own words, "softened" his pictorial expression. The subject matter is taken from Philostratus (*Eikones* I,6) who describes the games of cupids throughout the four seasons: throwing apples in spring, the fiery furnace of summer, Venus and Adonis taking their farewell in autumn and sleep in winter. Gian Lorenzo Bernini's self-portraits gaze penetratingly at the viewer from the centre of the wall. The first was painted when he was about twenty-five years old, when he sculpted the *David* and *Apollo and*

F. Albani, *Spring*, 1616-1617

F. Albani, *Summer*, 1616-1617

F. Albani, *Autumn*, 1616-1617

F. Albani, *Winter*, 1616-1617

Daphne. In the second Bernini painted himself with a fiery expression, circa 1630-1635, four years after executing the bust of Scipione Borghese, which is in the same room. This portrait is part of a double portrait with Costanza Bonarelli, which was described in Bernini's will as having already been cut in two. The third is the portrait of a youth with impressive features (c.1638), an unusual interpretation of childhood. These are all works in which the brushwork becomes increasingly spontaneous and seems to model the forms like a chisel sculpting marble.

This room also contains two portrait busts of *Cardinal Scipione Borghese*, executed by Gian Lorenzo Bernini around

Le Valentin, attrib., *St. Peter Freed from Prison*, c.1630

G. Reni, *Moses*, beginning of the 18th cent.

1632. In these works Bernini renders the jovial appearance of the Cardinal 'life-like and breathing', thus launching a new Roman Baroque style of marble portraiture featuring open and concave contours that interact with their surroundings (unlike Bernini's small, delicate *Bust of Paul V*, circa 1618, in the same room). Contemporary sources record that during the execution of the portrait bust a vein in the marble had caused a large crack to appear across the Cardinal's forehead. However, to everyone's surprise and in no time at all, Bernini succeeded in sculpting a second version of the bust, which differs from the first in a few important details: the jaunty position of his hat has been straightened and the folds of his cape are larger. When he was about seventeen Gian Lorenzo Bernini, in imitation of ancient sculpture, executed the group of *The Goat Amalthea with the Infant Jupiter and a Faun*.

Bernini had originally also designed the site (a mountain peak) for the *Equestrian Statue of Louis XIV*, the Sun King on a fiery steed, as can be seen from the preliminary sketch. The base supporting it today lacks the vertical thrust that would enhance the image of this absolute monarch. However, Bernini chose to make the features of Louis XIV resemble those of Alexander the Great. The original terracotta model is by Bernini himself, though the sculpture was executed by his pupils, since he was by then over seventy-three years old. However, the work did not meet with a favourable reception in Paris and Girardon transformed the group into a statue of Marcus Curtius, which was formerly transferred to Versailles and is now in the Louvre.

Room XV
Room of Aurora

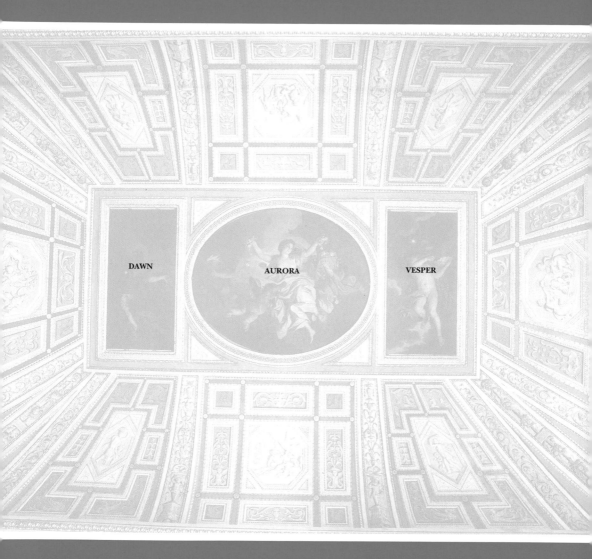

DAWN AURORA VESPER

Three central pictures: Domenico Corvi, 1782
Decorations: Giovanni Battista Marchetti
The medallions with the signs of the zodiac and the busts of philosophers
on the walls are also attributed to Domenico Corvi

Paintings: Jacopo Bassano: The Last Supper, 1546-47, no. 144; Sheep and Lamb, c.1560, no. 120 / Bernardino Licinio, The Family of the Artist's Brother, after 1535, no. 115 / Dosso Dossi: Gige and Candaule, c.1515, no. 225; Diana and Calisto, end of 1630s, no. 304; St. Cosmas and St. Damian, c.1534, no. 22; Madonna and Child, c.1525, no. 211; The Adoration of the Christ Child, c.1520, no. 220 / Scarsellino, Christ with His Disciples on the Road to Emmaus, c.1590, no. 226 / Girolamo Savoldo: Bust of a Youth, c.1530, no. 139; Tobias and the Angel, c.1530, no. 547 / Evangelista Dosso, attrib. to, The Nativity, c.1530, no. 215 / Battista di Dosso, The Holy Family with the Infant St. John the Baptist and an Angel, soon after 1510, no. 245.

G. Savoldo, *Tobias and the Angel*, c.1530

This room contains early 16th-century paintings from the Lombard and Veneto schools (which influenced Caravaggio's development of 'painting from nature'). The Ferrara school (see Room XI) is also represented with works by Dosso Dossi.

Jacopo Bassano's *Last Supper*, painted in 1542, is one of the masterpieces of 16th-century Italian painting. Instead of the elegant grouping of figures in Leonardo's painting, which inspired it, this dramatic scene features barefoot fishermen at the crucial moment when Christ asks who will betray him, and the light passing through a glass of wine stains the clean tablecloth red. Recent restoration has only now revealed the extraordinary original colours, which had been heavily painted over in the 19th century, when the emerald green and iridescent pinks and oranges were not in fashion. Jacopo Bassano's *Sheep and Lamb*, 1560, anticipated a new genre in painting, which was to become popular in the 17th century. The brilliant *Adoration of the Magi* (c.1576) is attributed to the elderly Jacopo and his son Francesco.

In *Tobias and the Angel*, the Brescian artist Giovanni Gerolamo Savoldo depicts the biblical episode in which a heavenly travelling companion tells the young Tobias to catch a fish and use its bile to cure his father's blindness. Savoldo has here produced a synthesis of his research into the effects of nature on the human figure, on drapery and on foliage, which appears to be pierced by light, and on the quality of colours seen in the distance, by adopting methods taught by Leonardo. A silvery light characterizes his paintings and this distinguishes him from other Venetian

G. Savoldo, *Bust of a Youth*, c.1530

J. Bassano, *Sheep and Lamb*, c.1560

D. Dossi, *Madonna and Child*, c.1525

D. Dossi, *Diana and Calisto*, c.1528

painters like Titian, who nonetheless influenced him, as did Lorenzo Lotto. Savoldo also became a reference point for the young Caravaggio, particularly in his half-length portraits of young men painted in a refined choice of colours and surrounded by strong chiaroscuro effects.

Dosso Dossi, the great Ferrarese master, belongs to a different world of mysterious and courtly fairy tales set in fantastic wild landscapes, with the addition of elements derived from northern European painting. Dossi's small *Madonna and Child* (c.1525) illustrates the per-

fect relationship between figures and nature: the golden rays from the halos are echoed in the leaves of the trees and the same shades of blue and green which modulate the Madonna's mantle are to be found in the different elements of the landscape. Dossi's *Diana and Calisto* (a nymph who had taken the vow of chastity, but was abandoned by Diana when the goddess discovered she had responded to Jupiter's love) was painted more than ten years later and reflects Raphael's influence. In his enigmatic work *St. Cosmas and St. Damian*, the patron saints of doctors, (1534-

J. Bassano, *The Last Supper*, 1546-1547

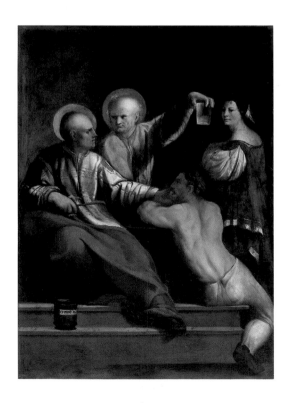

1542, from the hospital of S. Anna in Ferrara) Dossi recalls the monumentality and pathos of Michelangelo's figures. Bernardino Licino, a painter from Pordenone who was active in Venice, ennobles his highly unusual painting *Portrait of the Family of the Artist's Brother* (c.1533) by adding a famous ancient statue, the *Apollo Belvedere*, which is reduced in size and held in the artist's hand to underline his ancient culture and propensity for a classical style.

D. Dossi, *St. Cosmas and St. Damian*, 1534-1542

Room XVI
Room of Flora

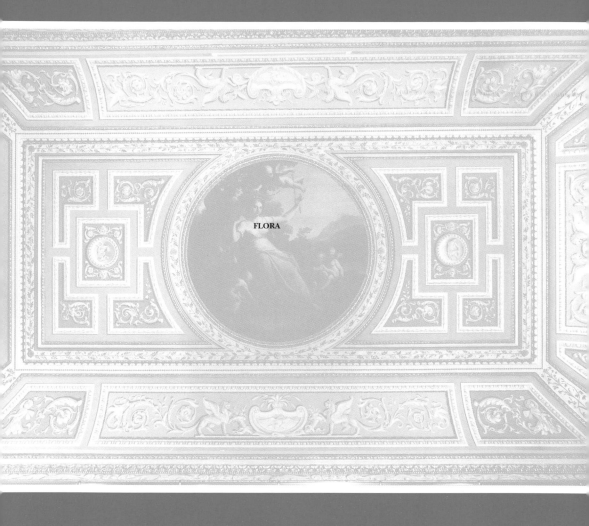

FLORA

Central tondo: Domenico de Angelis, 1785
Decorations: Giovanni Battista Marchetti
Fireplace: Luigi and Giuseppe Valadier, 1786

Paintings: Marco Pino, The Resurrection of Christ, 1569-76, no. 203 / Anonymous, An Apostle (St. Paul), beginning of 1560s, no. 37 / Marco Pino, attrib. to, An Apostle (St. Peter), beginning of 1560s, no. 46 / Pellegrino Tibaldi, The Adoration of the Christ Child, dated 1548, no. 415 /Jacopino del Conte, in the manner of, Lucretia, late 16th cent., no. 75 / Alessandro Allori, copy of Bronzino, Portrait of Cosimo I de' Medici, after 1560, no. 94 / Jacopino del Conte, Portrait of Vittoria Farnese, late 16th cent., no. 100 / Giorgio Vasari, The Nativity, c.1546, no. 271 / Jacopo Zucchi: Allegory of the Discovery of the New World, c.1585, no. 292; Allegory of the Creation, 1585, no. 293 / Jacopino del Conte, attrib. to, Cleopatra, mid-16th cent., no. 337.

This room houses 16th-century works in the manner of Michelangelo, whose famous small crucifix, now lost, was formerly in the Borghese Gallery. Giorgio Vasari, whose biography of Michelangelo and commitment to the Accademia delle Arti e del Disegno contributed to the creation of the legend of this great Florentine, painted the *Nativity* 'by night'. The elegant *Allegory of*

J. Zucchi, *Allegory of the Discovery of the New World*, c.1585

P. Tibaldi, *The Adoration of the Christ Child*, 1548

J. Zucchi, *Allegory of the Creation*, c.1585

G. Vasari, *The Nativity*, c.1546

the Creation and *Allegory of the Discovery of the New World* by Jacopo Zucchi (c.1585), formerly decorated Cardinal Ferdinando's *studiolo* in the nearby Villa Medici. In his *Adoration of the Christ Child*, 1548, Pellegrino Tibaldi surrounds the infant Jesus by a whirling crowd of worshipping figures reminiscent of the angels and the damned in the *Last Judgement* in the Sistine Chapel.

Similarly Marco Pino accentuates the power of his *St. Peter the Apostle* and the centrifugal displacement of the figures in his *Resurrection of Christ*. A particular aura of courtly splendid isolation characterizes the Florentine portraits of the period such as the painting of *Cosimo I de' Medici* by Alessandro Allori or Jacopino del Conte's portrait of *Vittoria Farnese*.

Room XVII
Room of the Story of the Count of Angers

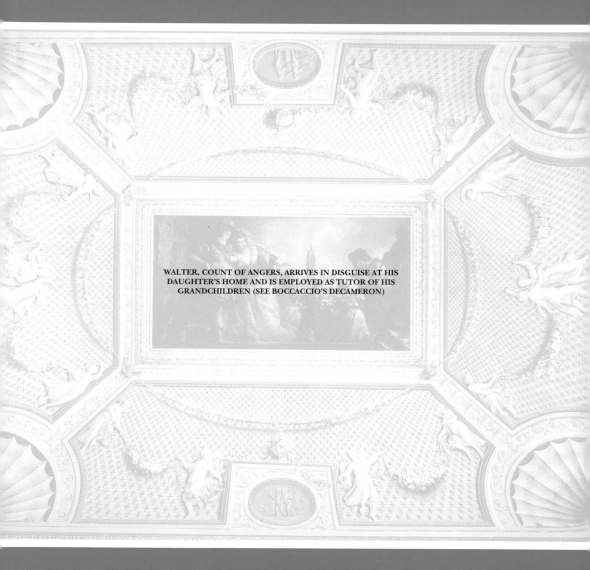

WALTER, COUNT OF ANGERS, ARRIVES IN DISGUISE AT HIS
DAUGHTER'S HOME AND IS EMPLOYED AS TUTOR OF HIS
GRANDCHILDREN (SEE BOCCACCIO'S DECAMERON)

Central painting: Giuseppe Cades, 1787
Two ovals and chiaroscuro figures: Thadeus Kuntze

Paintings: Wolfgang Heimbach, Man with a Lantern, 1645-50, no. 251 / Carlo Dolci: The Redeemer, c.1676, no. 306; Madonna and Child, mid-17th cent., no. 318 / Sassoferrato, Madonna and Child, c. mid 17th cent., no. 382 / Abraham van Cuylenborch, Diana Bathing, 1646, no. 490 / Sebastiano Conca, Virgin and Child with St. John Nepomucenus, a little before 1732, no. 560 / Michelangelo Cerquozzi: Bambocciade, c.1640, no. 249; Bambocciade, c.1640, no. 259 / Frans Francken the Younger, An Antique Dealer's Gallery, c.1615-20, no. 253 / Pieter De Hooch, Interior with Flautist, c.1670, no. 269 / Pieter Codde, Group of Guards, c.1635-39, no. 272 / Gillis Van Tilborgh, Interior of a Tavern, c.1650, no. 284 / Nicolas Lancret, A Dance, c.1720, no. 282 / Canaletto, attrib. to: The Colosseum, 1742-45, no. 540; The Basilica of Maxentius, 1742-45, no. 541 / Pompeo Batoni, Madonna and Child, c.1742, no. 542 / Corrado Giaquinto, The Annunciation, c.1753, no. 553 / Gaspare Landi: Portrait of Antonio Canova, 1806, no. 557; Self-Portrait, 1806, no. 558.

Sassoferrato, *Madonna and Child*, c.1650

This room contains 17th-century works considered to belong to a minor genre including those by the so-called *Bamboccianti*, named after Pieter van Laer, who was known as Il Bamboccio, who introduced this style of painting which often involved humourous depictions of everyday life. The *Bamboccianti* are here represented by two lively scenes by Michelangelo Cerquozzi. A special pictorial quality, reminiscent of Velazquez, distinguishes a small painting of a group of guards by Pieter Codde. There are also two small paintings of interiors by Wolfgang Heimbach, an interesting though little-known painter of candlelit scenes. The *Antique Dealer's Gallery* by Frans Francken the Younger, captures the atmosphere of such places at the beginning of the 17th century and shows a large

P. Batoni, *Madonna and Child*, c.1742

F. Francken the Younger, *An Antique Dealer's Gallery*, c.1615-1620

G. Landi, *Self-Portrait*, 1806

G. Landi, *Portrait of Canova*, 1806

display of paintings hanging in two rows. The few 18th-century works comprise a model by Sebastiano Conca for a large altarpiece, now lost, commissioned by Pope Benedict XIII for the basilica of S. Giovanni in Laterano in honour of the canonization of St. John Nepomucenus in 1729. An important sketch by Corrado Giaquinto (1753) was made for the altarpiece in the church at the hos-

pital of the Brothers of Piety in Graz. The *Madonna* by Pompeo Batoni (c.1742) can be compared with the 17th-century Madonnas by Sassoferrato and Carlo Dolci. Moving into the 19th century, a remarkable pair of portraits celebrates the friendship between Gaspare Landi the painter and the sculptor Antonio Canova by capturing their appearance in 1806 for posterity.

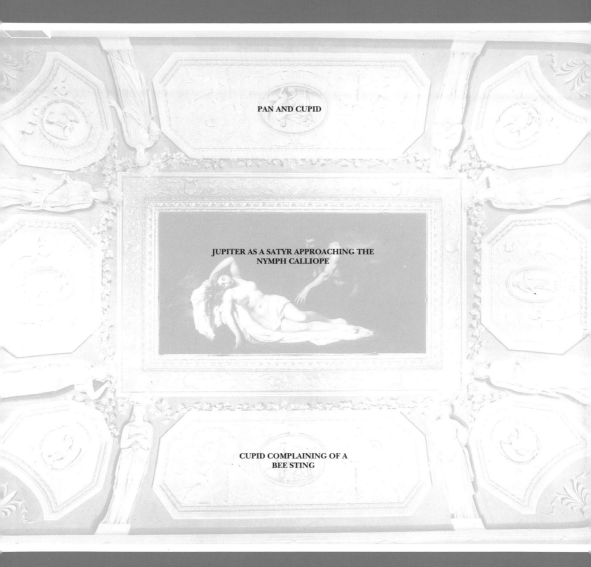

PAN AND CUPID

JUPITER AS A SATYR APPROACHING THE
NYMPH CALLIOPE

CUPID COMPLAINING OF A
BEE STING

Central painting: Benigne Gagneraux, 1787
Decorations: Vincenzo Berrettini

Paintings: Peter Paul Rubens: The Deposition, c.1602, no. 411; Susanna and the Elders, 1605-7, no. 277 / Anton Van Dyck, in the manner of, Christ Crucified, early 17th cent., no. 268 / Marten Mandekens, The Visitation, c.1638, no. 27 / Pietro da Cortona, Portrait of Marcello Sacchetti, c.1626, no. 364 /Andrea Sacchi, Portrait of Monsignor Clemente Merlini. 1630-31, no. 376 / Sisto Badalocchio, attrib. to, The Entombment of Christ, beginning of 17th cent., no. 43.

P. P. Rubens, *The Deposition*, 1602

In this room two masterpieces typify the changes in the style of Roman Baroque portraits. Andrea Sacchi's *Portrait of Monsignor Clemente Merlini,* painted in circa 1630, shows this sharp-witted jurist, Latin scholar and Epicurean, with his books casually displayed behind him, turning to look directly at the spectator. Pietro da Cortona depicts his patron, the cultured *Marcello Sacchetti* (1626), in a spontaneous pose in front of a gilded table bearing his coat of arms.

Peter Paul Rubens, the genius of European Baroque, painted his *Deposition* (1602) during his first stay in Rome. Rubens provides us with an extraordinary interpretation of the theme of the incarnation of the divine and human nature of Christ, suspended between death and potential future life. All the shades of the spectrum of light are apparent in the flesh tones, with an opalescence that develops that mother of pearl quality first introduced by Federico Barrocci (see also the contrast between the living hand of Mary Magdalen and the bluish tinge of Christ's as compared with Raphael's painting in Room IX). The impact made on Rubens by Roman statuary can be seen in the antique altar with sacrifice scenes, but above all in the strong sculptural high relief of the figures. The dense chromatic texture of the composition owes much Titian's later works, while the airy vibrato and gentle rhythms echo Correggio's achievements. The light unexpectedly bursting through the dark area

S. Badalocchio, *The Entombment of Christ,* c.1610

A. Sacchi, *Portrait of Monsignor Clemente Merlini*, c. 1630

Pietro da Cortona, *Marcello Sacchetti*, c.1626

of the painting provides evidence that Rubens competed in an original way with the chiaroscuro experiments of his contemporary Caravaggio.

Similarly in his *Susanna Bathing* (1606) with the elders spying on her, Rubens dramatically accentuates the 'expressions' of those looking in opposite directions, which was a primary element in Baroque painting.

The important *Entombment of Christ* dating from the first decade of the 17th century may be attributed to Sisto Badalocchio. Here human participation in the event has become the main focus. A comparison with Raphael's *Deposition* (Room IX), which inspired it, reveals how the painter insisted on the emotions as reflected in natural movements, and was influenced both by Dürer's prints and antique sculpture.

Room XIX
Room of Paris and Helen

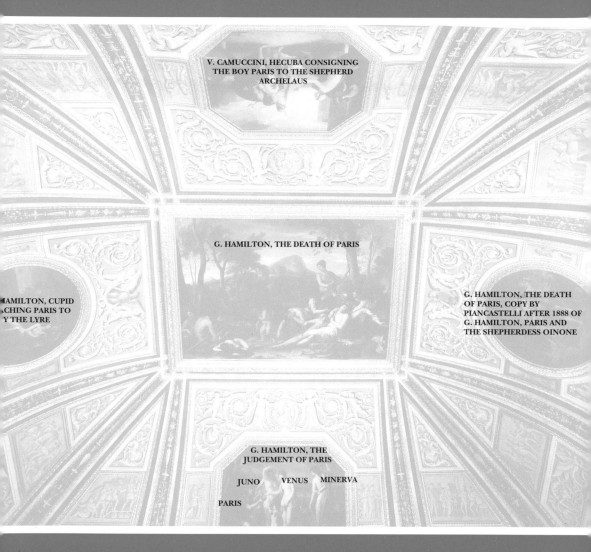

V. CAMUCCINI, HECUBA CONSIGNING
THE BOY PARIS TO THE SHEPHERD
ARCHELAUS

G. HAMILTON, THE DEATH OF PARIS

HAMILTON, CUPID
CHING PARIS TO
Y THE LYRE

G. HAMILTON, THE DEATH
OF PARIS, COPY BY
PIANCASTELLI AFTER 1888 OF
G. HAMILTON, PARIS AND
THE SHEPHERDESS OINONE

G. HAMILTON, THE
JUDGEMENT OF PARIS

JUNO   VENUS   MINERVA

PARIS

Pictures transferred to the ceiling: G. Hamilton, V. Camuccini and L. Piancastelli
Yellow marble reliefs of Apollo, Mars, Venus and Jupiter: Vincenzo Pacetti

Sculptures: G. Finelli, Bust of Cardinal Domenico Gimasi, c.1639 no. CCLXX / D. Guidi, attrib. to, Portrait of Felice Zacchia Rondinini, c.1660 no. CCLXVII / Roman sculpture, Young Moor with a Girl and a Dog, end of 16th cent. no. LVII / 2 Vases with handles in the shape of serpents by Silvio Calci da Velletri (from a drawing by A. Algardi), 1638, no. CCXIX.
Paintings: Annibale Carracci, The Laughing Youth, 1583-85, no. 83 / Federico Barocci: Aeneas' Flight from Troy, dated 1598, no. 68; St Jerome, c.1598, no. 403 / Fede Galizia, Judith with the Head of Holofernes, dated 1601, no. 165 / Simone Cantarini: The Holy Family with the Infant St. John the Baptist, c.1642, no. 549; St. John the Baptist, 1625-35, no. 357 / Giovan Francesco Romanelli, A Sibyl, 1640-50, no. 51 / Domenichino: Diana, 1616-17, no. 53; A Sibyl, 1616-17, no. 55 / Agostino Carracci, The Ecstasy of St. Catherine, end of 16th cent., no. 58 / Gaspare Celio, The Battle of Furius Camillus, after 1612, no. 344 / Giovanni Lanfranco, Norandino and Lucina Discovered by the Ogre, 1619-25, no. 16 / Sassoferrato copy of Titian, The Three Ages of Man, early 17th cent., no. 346 / Pietro Paolo Bonzi, called Il Gobbo dei Carracci, Head of a Satyr Crowned with Vine Leaves, early 17th cent., 44x30 cm., no. 160.

Domenichino, *A Sybil*, 1616-1617

This room brings together works by Baroque painters and their immediate predecessors.

Federico Barrocci's *Aeneas' Flight from Troy* with Anchises, his son Ascanius and his wife Creusa is the second version painted in 1598 of a picture executed ten years earlier for Emperor Rudolf II of Austria. Cardinal Giuliano della Rovere presented Cardinal Scipione with this second version, which entered the Borghese collection before 1613. It was this painting that inspired Cardinal Scipione to commission a large marble group on the same subject from Gian Lorenzo Bernini (see Room VI). Both works were displayed in Room III in the Borghese Gallery together with an allegorical painting of *Rome* by Cigoli. The myth of Aeneas, ancestor

F. Barocci, *St. Jerome*, c.1598

F. Barocci, *Aeneas' Flight from Troy*, 1598

of Romulus and Remus, referred to the birth of Rome and thus confirmed the Borghese family's high status in the city. Barrocci's many drawings of nature led him to achieve a spontaneity and naturalness in movement, colour and airy effects, and a silvery luminosity that was to influence the 17th-century masters, particularly Rubens. Never before had flames been painted so close to, with an energy suggesting even the crackle of the fire, from which Ascanius seems to be protecting himself by covering his ears. But the human delicacy of Barrocci's anti-heroic and anti-rhetorical figures was not to be really appreciated in Rome, because it could not compete with the classical antique statuary.

In Barrocci's *St. Jerome* of the same period, recent restoration has revealed a lion, sleeping like a large cat in the background; it had been hidden under thick layers of paint that had darkened with age.

In his *Diana* (1616-1617) Domenichino revived antique themes and the depiction of nymphs. The subject derives from Virgil's *Aeneid* (V, 485) where warriors are described competing in an archery contest and shooting a tree with their first arrow, a ribbon with their second and a falling bird with their third. It was probably Mons. Giovanni Battista Agucchi, major theorist and adviser on iconography at the time, who suggested transposing the subject matter into the realm of the nymphs led by Diana. The archery theme was adopted as a

Domenichino, *Diana*, 1616-1617

G. Lanfranco, *Norandino and Lucina Discovered by the Ogre*, c.1624

metaphor for shrewd arguments that hit the mark, which was topical at the time, as the dedication of the *Dicerie sacre* by the poet Giovan Battista Marino to Pope Paul V indicates. In capturing nature in clear compositions that predominate over the use of colour, Domenichino nonetheless adopts Venetian tones now and then in the flowing draperies, and there are extraordinary passages from green to yellow, white to blue and various shades of purple. But what opens up a new chapter in the rendering of atmosphere are his gradual and calculated changes in tone towards the pale blue mountains by using increasingly subtle glazings, which indicate a new interest in Leonardo's theories on aerial perspective (studied and taught by the

Theatine monk Matteo Zaccolini, who taught Domenichino perspective in the 1620s). Chromatic modulations also characterize the *Sybil* by Domenichino, who was also an expert in music. The figure is depicted with a viola da gamba and a music book, because traditionally in antiquity sybils sang their prophecies to the accompaniment of musical instruments.

Lanfranco's large painting of *Norandino and Lucina Discovered by the Ogre* was commissioned by Cardinal Scipione for his villa at Frascati, at the time when the artist was working on *The Council of the Gods* in the loggia of the Villa Borghese (1624, Room XIV). It depicts an episode from Ariosto's *Orlando Furioso* (XII, 23 ff.), in which Norandino, King of Damascus and his bride Lucina are shipwrecked on the Ogre's island while on their honeymoon. They attempt to escape from the cave, but Lucina is discovered. Lanfranco's figures move theatrically and are rendered with rapid brushstrokes. The dense colour of the classical landscape make Lanfranco far-removed from the delicate glazing of his r i v a l Domenichino. Capturing a moment of laughter in painting is not an easy task, but the young Annibale Carracci succeeds in his sketchy portrait of a *L a u g h i n g Youth*, oil on paper, dating from circa 1583. Though this is a small work its spontaneity is extraordinarily modern and anticipates the portraits by Bernini and Velazquez fifty years later. Carraci's interest in caricature is well known, but here he seeks to capture the boy's expression as it is in real life. This is a portrait of an actor, as can be seen from the hat, which was used for the B o l o g n e s e mask of the 'doctor'. Its spontaneity is enhanced by the strong square cut of the bust and the charcoal lines and brush-strokes, which reflect the speed of execution.

A. Carracci, *The Laughing Youth*, 1583

Room XX
Room of Psyche, formerly of the Centaur

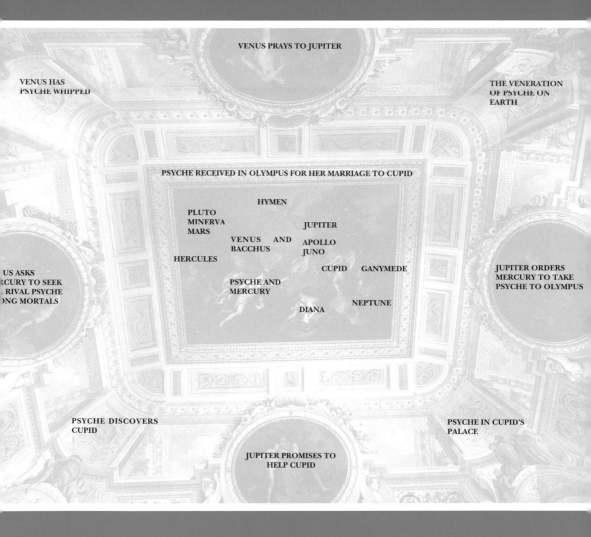

VENUS PRAYS TO JUPITER

VENUS HAS
PSYCHE WHIPPED

THE VENERATION
OF PSYCHE ON
EARTH

PSYCHE RECEIVED IN OLYMPUS FOR HER MARRIAGE TO CUPID

HYMEN

PLUTO
MINERVA
MARS

JUPITER

VENUS AND
BACCHUS

APOLLO
JUNO

HERCULES

CUPID   GANYMEDE

PSYCHE AND
MERCURY

DIANA

NEPTUNE

US ASKS
RCURY TO SEEK
. RIVAL PSYCHE
ONG MORTALS

JUPITER ORDERS
MERCURY TO TAKE
PSYCHE TO OLYMPUS

PSYCHE DISCOVERS
CUPID

PSYCHE IN CUPID'S
PALACE

JUPITER PROMISES TO
HELP CUPID

Pictures transferred to the ceiling, putti and sphinxes: Pietro Novelli, 1781
Illusionist decorations: Giovanni Battista Marchetti
Fireplace: Agostino Penna, 1782

Sculpture: Bronze Portrait of a Youth, perhaps Geta, c.196 AD, no. CCLII, restored by Gio. Battista della Porta, 16th cent.
Paintings: Antonello da Messina, Portrait of a Man, 1474-75, no. 396 / Bartolomeo Montagna, The Young Christ, c.1502, no. 430 / Vittore Carpaccio, attrib. to, Portrait of a Woman, c.1495-1500, no. 450 / Marco Basaiti, attrib. to: Adam, after 1504, no. 129; Eve, after 1504, no. 131 / Giovanni Bellini, Madonna and Child, c.1510, no. 176 / Lorenzo Lotto, Madonna and Child with St. Flavian and St. Onophrius, dated 1508, no. 193 / Jacopo Palma il Vecchio: The Holy Conversation with St. Barbara, St. Christine and Two Worshippers, 1510-20, no. 157; Portrait of a Youth, dated 1510, no.445 / Titian: Sacred and Profane Love, c.1514, no. 147; Venus Blindfolding Cupid, c.1565, no. 170; St. Dominic, c.1565, no. 188; The Scourging of Christ, c.1560, no. 194 / Giorbione, attrib. to, Portrait of a Man, 16th cent. no. 82 / Veronese, St. Anthony Preaching to the Fish, c.1580, no. 101 / Jacopo Palma il Vecchio, attrib. to, Lucretia, 1525-28, no. 106 / Giorgione, attrib. to: The Singer with a Flute, no. 130; The Impassioned Singer, 16th cent., no. 132, / Veronese, St. John the Baptist Preaching, c.1562, no. 137.

Antonello da Messina, *Portrait of a Man*, c.1475

This room containing a valuable bronze statue of a boy from the Antonine family (2nd century AD) is devoted to the masters of Venetian Renaissance painting. Tradition has it that when Antonello da Messina returned from Flanders he introduced the technique of oil painting to Venice. He was also influenced by northern painting in his Sicilian search for the individual character of people and things, as is evident from the extraordinary *Portrait of a Man*, circa 1475. His objective and incisive analysis of forms combines Piero della Francesa's stereometric achievements, Mantegna's use of perspective in his busts and Venetian colour. Its present state of preservation shows that the highlighting on the red robe, has now become blackened by the lead base of the white pigment.

Giovanni Belloni, father of Venetian painting, according to A. Venturi "knew how to draw from his lyre only the most delicate harmonies", which can still be seen in the *Madonna and Child* painted around 1510, when he was 84 years old. In the 17th century the two panels of *Adam* and *Eve* were also attributed to this great master, though more recent critics attribute them to Marco Basaiti. Their composition was inspired by a

L. Lotto, *Madonna and Child, with St. Flavian and St Onophrius*, 1508

G. Bellini, *Madonna and Child*, c.1510

famous print by A. Dürer dating from 1504, in which the figures are set among tall trees. Cardinal Scipione's collection had to include works by Giorgione, to whom the famous *Singers* were attributed. They sing with an air of Baroque pathos surrounded by strong chiaroscuro effects, which in fact have induced many experts today to date them to the beginning of the 17th century.

In the *Madonna and Child with St. Flavian and St. Onophrius*, 1508, the young Lorenzo Lotto is influenced by Dürer, who when in Venice in 1506 had painted sacred paintings of great chromatic intensity and asymmetrical composition (see the *Madonna of the Thistle*, now in the Berlin Museum, with her knee right on the edge of the picture and the fleeting profile of the Infant Jesus). Lotto's wild St. Onophrius is based on the man with the long beard in Dürer's *Christ among the Doctors* (now in the Thyssen Collection, Lugano). In Palma il Vecchio's *Sacred Conversation*, 1510, depicting St. Barbara, St. Justina and two donors, A. Longhi has described "the sharply defined islands of colour that don't blend, but almost seem to float" which we also believe to have derived from Dürer's use of form and colour in Venice (see the *Madonna of the Rosary*, now in Prague).

The extraordinary beauty of the Venetian fabrics already to be found in the work of Palma il Vecchio is brought to unrivalled perfection by Paolo Veronese. In the *St. John the Baptist Preaching* (c.1562), which heralds the coming of Christ, the figures are wrapped in magnificent oriental silk robes and three are wearing turbans. Their differing reactions to the sermon

V. Carpaccio, *Portrait of a Woman*, 1495-1500

Giorgione, attrib. to, *The Impassioned Singer*, 16th cent.

Titian, *Venus Blindfolding Cupid*, c.1565

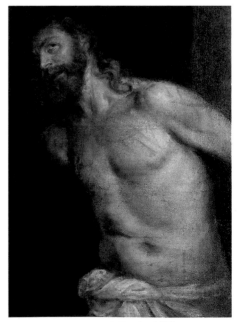

Titian, *St. Dominic*, c.1565   Titian, *The Scourging of Christ*, c.1560

are reflected in their facial expressions. The skilful composition of the painting creates a balance between the weight of the group of figures on the right and the perspective on the left. Twenty years later in the *St. Anthony Preaching to the Fish* the same spatial tension dominates the vast expanse of sea.

Titian's *Venus Blindfolding Cupid* (c.1565) evokes Cupid's blind power as his mother, the cosmic divinity, blindfolds him. His brother is intent on observing the large number of arrows or fatal darts of love (a metaphor for amorous glances) the nymph is carrying. The rapid brush-strokes of Titian's mature pictorial technique when seen close to seem to break up the forms but from a distance they acquire an extra-

Veronese, *St. John the Baptist Preaching*, c.1562

Veronese, *St. Anthony Preaching to the Fish*, c.1580

Titian, *Sacred and Profane Love*, 1514

ordinary modelled quality and create a chromatic texture that blends the background and figures in a 'Venetian' harmony of colours. In the 17th century this style influenced Velazquez, Rubens, van Dyck and Caravaggio, as can be seen from a comparison between Titian's *St. Dominic* (1565) and Caravaggio's *David with the Head of Goliath*, both exhibited in Room VIII.

Sacred and Profane Love, Titian's masterpiece painted when he was about twenty-five to celebrate the marriage of the Venetian Nicolò Aurelio (coat of arms on the sarcophagus) and Laura Bagarotto in 1514. The bride dressed in white sitting beside Cupid is assisted by Venus in person. The figure with the vase of jewels symbolizes 'fleeting happiness on earth' and the one bearing the burning flame of God's love symbolizes 'eternal happiness in heaven'. The title is the result of a late 18th-century interpretation of the painting, which gives a moralistic reading of the nude figure, whereas the artist intended this to be an exaltation of both earthly and heavenly love. In fact in the Neoplatonic philosophy that Titian and his circle believed in contemplating the beauty of the creation led to an awareness of the divine perfection of the order of the cosmos. In this painting of love in the open countryside Titian has surpassed the delicate lyrical poetry of Giovanni Bellini or Giorgione and attributes a classical grandeur to his figures. In 1899, the Rothschilds offered to buy this world famous work at a price that was higher than the estimated value of the Villa Borghese and all its works of art (4,000,000 Lire as opposed to 3,600,000 Lire). However, Titian's *Sacred and Profane Love* has remained and virtually become the symbol of the Borghese Gallery itself.

Titian, *Sacred and Profane Love*, detail, 1514

Selected Bibliography

Index of Names

The essential catalogues of the Borghese Gallery are:
of the sculptures: I. Faldi, *Galleria Borghese, Le sculture dal secolo XVI al XIX*, Rome, 1954 with bibliog.;
of the paintings: P. della Pergola, *Galleria Borghese, I dipinti*, 2. vols., Rome, 1955, 1959 with bibliog.;
of the 18th-century decorations: S. Petereit Guicciardi, *Das Casino Borghese, Dekoration und Inhalt*, Diss. Vienna , 2 vols., 1983;
of the antique statuary: P. Moreno, *Museo e Galleria Borghese, La collezione archeologica*, Rome, 1980.

F. Noack, 'Kunstplege und Kunstbesitz der Familie Borghese, in *Repertorium fur Kunstwissenschaft* 50, 1929, pp. 191-231
L. Ferrara, 'La stanza di Elena e Paride, in *Rivista dell'Istituto Nazionale di Archeologia e Storia dell'Arte* n. s. III, 1954, pp. 242-256.
R. Longhi, 'Precisioni nelle Gallerie Italiane, La R. Galleria Borghese' (1928) reprinted in R. Longhi, *Opere complete II, Saggi e ricerche*, Florence, 1967, pp. 265 - 366
C. H. Heilmann, 'Die Einsterhungsgeschichte der Villa Borghese in Rom', *Munchner Jahrbuch fur Bildende Kunst*, III, 24, 1973, pp. 97-158
W. Reinhard, 'Papstfinanz und Nepotismus unter Paul V' (1605-1621), in *Papste und Papstum*, ed. G. Dengler, Stuttgart, 1974
P. Arizzoli - Clémentel, 'Charles Percier et la salle égyptienne de la villa Borghèse', in *Académie de France a Rome II, Colloque tenue à la Villa Médicis*, Rome, 1976, pp. 1-32
Le collezioni della Galleria Borghese Roma ed. S. Staccioli and P. Moreno, Touring Club Italiano, Milan, 1981
V. Reinhardt, *Kardinal Scipione Borghese* (1605-1633), Vermogen, Finanzen und sozialer Aufstieg, Tübingen, 1984
B. Di Gaddo, *Villa Borghes, Il Giardino e le Architetture*, Rome, 1985
M. Winner, 'Bernini the Sculptor and the Classical Heritage in his

Early Years: Praxiteles', Bernini's and Lanfranco's Pluto and Proserpina, in *Romisches Jahrbuch fur Kunstgeschichte* 22, 1985, pp. 193-235
B. Di Gaddo, *Villa Borghese, Il Giardino e le Architetture*, Rome, 1985, p. 58
K. Herrmann Fiore, 'Il colore delle facciate di Villa Borghese nel contesto delle dominanti coloristiche dell'edilizia romana intorno al 1600', in: *Bollettino d'arte* 48, 1988, pp.10-93 and 'Testimonianze storiche sull'evangelizzazione del Oriente...nella Sala Regia del Quirinale', in *Da Sendai a Roma, Un'ambasceria giapponese a Paolo V*, exhibition catalogue, Rome, 1990, pp. 9-103
C. Paul, 'Mariano Rossi's Camillus Fresco in the Borghese Gallery', in *The Art Bulletin* LXXIV, 1992, pp. 297-326
R. Gonzàlez - 'Palacios, La stanza del Gladiatore', in *Antologia di Belle Arti*, 43-47, 1993, pp. 5-33
A. Campitelli, *Il parco di Villa Borghese*, Rome, 1993
Galleria Borghese, ed. A. Coliva, ENEL, Rome, 1994, with bibliog.
E. Fumagalli, *Palazzo Borghese committenza e decorazione privata*, Rome 1994 con bibliog.
A. Antinori, *Scipione Borghese e l'architettura, programmi progetti cantieri alle soglie dell'età barocca*, Rome, 1995
A. Gonzàles - 'Palacios, The Stanza di Apollo e Dafne in the Villa Borghese', in *The Burlington Magazine*, August 1995, pp. 529-549
K. Kalveram, 'Die Antikensammlung des Kardinals Scipione Borghese', *Romische Studien der Bibliotheca Hertziana*, Worms, 1995

***

Agricola Gioacchino 32
Aguatti Cesare 41
Albani Francesco 89
Alberti Alberto 11
Albertinelli Mariotto 86
Alfani Tiberio 70
Algardi A. 14, 41, 73
Allori Alessandro 102
Angeletti Pietro 37
Antonello da Messina 119
Asprucci A. 8, 16, 41, 46, 52

Bachiacca 86
Badalocchio Sisto 110
Baglione G. 3, 16, 59
Barocci Federico 109, 113, 114
Basaiti Marco 119
Bassano Francesco 95
Bassano Jacopo 16, 95
Bassetti Marcantonio 89
Batoni Pompeo 106
Baur W. 21, 64
Beccafumi D. 83
Bellini Giovanni 124
Bernini G.L. 5, 14, 16, 26, 30, 32, 37, 41, 43, 46, 49, 50, 90, 91, 92, 113, 116
Bernini P. 14, 22, 25, 26, 30, 49
Bonvicini Nicola 46
Bracci Pietro 14
Brescianino 73
Brill P. 64
Bronzino 77
Brunetti A. 25

Caccianiga Francesco 32
Cades Giuseppe 8
Canina L. 8, 14, 16, 22
Canova 14, 16, 29, 106
Caravaggio 5, 15, 16, 17, 57, 59, 62, 89, 95, 97, 110, 124
Cardelli L. 37, 43
Carracci Annibale 16, 32, 89, 116
Carracciolo Battistello 32
Carradori Francesco 8, 25
Cavaceppi B. 15
Cavalier d' Arpino 14, 16, 17, 57, 59
Cerquozzi Michelangelo 105
Cesari Giuseppe. See Cavalier d' Arpino
Cigoli 59, 113
Codde Pieter 105
Conca Sebastiano 106
Conca Tommaso 8, 52, 57
Cordier Nicolas 5, 14, 73

Correggio 8, 15, 75
Corvi Domenico 8, 89
Costa Lorenzo 86
Cranach 16, 73

d' Oggiono Marco 83
dal Colle Raffaellino 67, 70
de Angelis Domenico 8, 29, 41
de Chalôns Simon 83
del Conte Jacopino. 102
del Sarto Andrea 75, 86
del Vaga Perin 67
della Porta Giovan Battista 14
della Porta Guglielmo 38
della Porta Tommaso 14
Deruet C. 15, 38
Dirk van Baburen 59
Dolci Carlo 15, 106
Domenichino 5, 8, 15, 114, 115, 116
Dossi Dosso 15, 37, 80, 95, 97, 98
Ducrot Giuseppe 22
Duquesnoy F. 14
Dürer 67, 110, 121

Elsheimer 89

Finelli Giuliano 14
Fontana Lavinia 15
Fra Bartolomeo 67, 86
Fracanzano 15
Francia Francesco 86
Francken Frans the Younger 106
Furttenbach Joseph 12

Garofalo 80
Giampietrino 83
Giani Felice 8
Giaquinto Corrado 106
Giorgione 124
Girardon 92
Girolamo da Carpi 75
Govaert van Schayck 64
Granacci 86
Guercino 15, 89
Guerrieri Giovan Francesco 15, 89

Hackert 15
Hamilton Gavin 8, 15
Heimbach Wolfgang 105
Holbein 67
Honthorst 89
Houdon Giovanni Antonio 14, 38

Kress Master of Landscapes 86

Laboureur M. 8, 25, 43
Landi Gaspare 15, 106
Lanfranco G. 4, 15, 17, 89, 115, 116
Leonardo 67, 69, 83, 95, 115
Licinio Bernardino 98
Lippi Annibale 11
Lysippus 21, 32, 52, 57
Longhi il Vecchio 7
Longhi R. 83, 84, 86
Lotto Lorenzo 84, 97, 121

Machuca 67
Master of the Sforza Altarpiece 83
Manetti Rutilio 32
Mantegna 119
Marchetti Giovanni Battista 8, 29, 32, 37, 41, 52, 57
Maron, Anton von 8
Maturino 11
Mazzolino 80
Memling 86
Mengs 49
Michelangelo 11, 14, 22, 32, 50, 70, 98, 100
Mola 89

Nicolò dell' Abate 75
Novelli Pietro Antonio 8

Ortolano 80
Ottini Pasquale 89

Pacetti V. 8, 25, 46, 49
Palma il Giovane 64
Palma il Vecchio 121
Passignano 16
Pecheux Laurent 49
Penna Agostino 8
Perugino 67, 69
Peters Wenzel 8, 15, 25
Piero della Francesca 69, 119
Piero di Cosimo 67
Pietro da Cortona 109
Pino Marco 102
Pinturicchio 67
Piranesi 52
Polycles 46
Polycletus 22
Polidoro 11
Pontormo 86
Ponzio Flaminio 3, 4, 7, 12, 13, 21

Praxiteles 26
Provenzale Marcello 15, 64

Raphael 8, 14, 15, 52, 67, 69, 70, 97, 109, 110
Rainaldi Girolamo 12
Reni Guido 5, 15, 59, 89
Righi T. 25
Romano Giulio 16, 67, 70, 80
Rossi Mariano 8, 25
Rubens 5, 15, 41, 50, 89, 109, 110, 114, 124

Sacchi Andrea 109
Salaì 83
Salimei L. 25
Saraceni C. 4
Sassoferrato 15, 106
Savino da Montepulciano Domenico 13
Savoldo Giovanni Gerolamo 95, 97
Schauffelein H. 67
Sodoma 83
Solario A. 83
Susini Antonio 14, 43

Tassi A. 4
Thorvaldsen Berthel 57
Tibaldi Pellegrino 102
Titian 32, 57, 97, 109, 123, 124
Turchi Alessandro 89

Ubertini Francesco. See Bachiacca
Unterberger Cristoforo 8

Valadier Luigi 8, 14, 43
Valentin 89
van Dyck 124
van Laer Pieter 105
van Santen G.. See Vasanzio
Vasanzio 12, 13
Vasari Giorgio 100
Velazquez 105, 116, 124
Veronese Paolo 121
Verrocchio 67

Wallbaum Matthias 38

Zaccolini Matteo 115
Zeuxis 59
Zuccari Federico 38
Zuccari Taddeo 38
Zucchi Jacopo 102

Printed July 1997
by
Conti Tipocolor s.r.l. - Florence